D0857508

Lebanon: *Poems of Love and War*

❧

Liban: *Poèmes d'amour et de guerre*

Middle East Literature in Translation

Michael Beard *and* Adnan Haydar, *Series Editors*

Lebanon

Poems of Love and War

Liban

Poèmes d'amour et de guerre

Nadia Tuéni

A Bilingual Anthology

Edited by Christophe Ippolito

Translated from the French by
Samuel Hazo *and* Paul B. Kelley

Editions Dar An-Nahar

Syracuse University Press

English translations © 2006 by Syracuse University Press
Syracuse, New York 13244–5160
Original text copyrighted by Fondation Nadia Tuéni and
Editions Dar An-Nahar
La Prose: Oeuvres complètes of Nadia Tuéni © 1986 by Dar An-Nahar
Les Oeuvres poétiques complètes of Nadia Tuéni © 1986 by Dar An-Nahar
All Rights Reserved

First Edition 2006
06   07   08   09   10   11   6   5   4   3   2   1

Copublication with Les Editions Dar An-Nahar, Beirut, Lebanon, with the
Nadia Tuéni Foundation.

Liban: Vingt poèmes pour un amour/Lebanon: Twenty Poems for One Love,
translated by Samuel Hazo, was previously published by Byblos Press, New
York, in 1990.

The paper used in this publication meets the minimum requirements of
American National Standard for Information Sciences—Permanence of
Paper for Printed Library Materials, ANSI Z39.48–1984.∞™

Library of Congress Cataloging-in-Publication Data
Tuéni, Nadia.
[Liban. English & French]
Lebanon : poems of love and war = Liban : poèmes d'amour et de guerre /
Nadia Tuéni ; a bilingual anthology edited by Christophe Ippolito ;
translated from the French by Samuel Hazo and Paul B. Kelley.— 1st ed.
p. cm. — (Middle East literature in translation)
title: Liban.
Includes bibliographical references.
ISBN 0-8156-3090-5 (hardcover : alk. paper) — ISBN 0-8156-0816-0
(pbk. : alk. paper)
I. Title: Liban. II. Ippolito, Christophe, 1963– III. Hazo, Samuel John IV.
Kelley, Paul B., 1967– V. Tuéni, Nadia. Archives sentimentales d'une guerre
au Liban. English & French. Selections. VI. Title. VII. Series.
PQ3979.2.T84L5313 2005
841'.914—dc22   2005033150

Manufactured in the United States of America

Once upon a time in Lebanon,

freedom had a name,

and it was Gebran's.

I dedicate this book to Gebran Tuéni,

cowardly assassinated on December 12, 2005,

and to those who fought for freedom.

CHRISTOPHE IPPOLITO

Contents

Archives sentimentales d'une guerre au Liban: Choix de poèmes

Sentimental Archives of a War in Lebanon: A Selection

Introduction

CHRISTOPHE IPPOLITO

❧There are many ways to reflect poetically on a war: in French, the poets Ronsard, Éluard, Char, to name a few, have done so in a unique way, seeking through the evils of pain and disaster a deeper knowledge of the human experience. The poems selected for the present bilingual edition are haunted by the Lebanese war because they come from the two collections that were published by Francophone poet Nadia Tuéni (1935–1983) in 1979 and 1982 respectively during the civil war in Lebanon, a war that continued from 1975 to 1989. These volumes offer two dramatically different poetic answers to war: the earlier collection transcends famous Lebanese locales and serves as the symbolic incarnation of the land's eternal essence; the latter work—illuminated at its outset by nostalgic memories but transmuted into a prophetic tone by its end— deals with the daily reality of war as perceived by the senses. Although the first collection, *Liban: Vingt poèmes pour un amour,* is here presented in its entirety as it was translated in English in 1990, I am honored to present to the English-speaking public the first English translation of twenty selected poems of the widely celebrated 1982 collection *Archives sentimentales d'une guerre au Liban (Sentimental Archives of a War in Lebanon).* This collection of poems addresses themes on love and war in Beirut from the perspective of a dying woman; it is a short volume of poems about a terrible war, but it is also a book whose main theme is love.

Nadia Tuéni, as Syrine C. Hout shows in her essay, "Home, Politics, and Exile" in the present volume, was a woman at the confluence of two cultures: Western and Middle Eastern. Although not a feminist in the strict sense of the term (one may find her lectures on women in *Oeuvres complètes, La Prose*), she has reflected on femininity and on the female condition, as well as on women poets.

And, although not an "engaged" writer in the Sartrean sense, her poems have nonetheless captured the tragic political situation of the late seventies and early eighties in Lebanon, and she probably has done this better than many of her counterparts. Today, Tuéni's poetry is generally viewed as a national treasure, and it is not uncommon to meet young Lebanese who know some of her poems by heart. The poems of *Liban: Vingt poèmes pour un amour,* dedicated to Lebanese children as well as to her daughter Nayla who she prematurely lost to cancer, are now widely read in Lebanese schools. These poems present symbolic images ("paintings," some have said) of Lebanese cities and regions and develop both the historical and mythical dimensions present in the imaginary constructions of these locales and their implications for the future of Lebanon. To offer but a few examples, Beirut is represented not only as a crossroads between East and West and as a courtesan of the arts but also as the last "sanctuary" of liberty in the East, while the Shuf mountains are depicted as a close, secretive, and mystical universe where resistance and reserve are keywords. Throughout the collection, the poet's distinctive, subjective, and prophetic voice articulates a unifying role for a country divided by civil war, and it celebrates the continuous harmony of opposites as constituting the essence of the land. In a Druze perspective, this voice speaks to us from a realm halfway between reality and pure reason—a spiritual world, an internalized, imaginary hinterland. I had to make a choice for the second collection: although this selection was chosen purely from an aesthetic point of view, I have tried whenever possible to maintain the collection's unity by presenting a balanced, albeit arbitrary, choice of poems among the three parts (the past, present, and future) and forty poems that constitute the entire *Archives sentimentales d'une guerre au Liban.* Only twenty poems of *Archives sentimentales* have been selected, and I refer the reader to the Jad Hatem edition for the complete collection in the original French. My chief hope one day is to see the complete poems of *Archives sentimentales d'une guerre au*

Liban and beyond that *all* of Nadia Tuéni's works, prose and poetry, translated into English. May this happen soon!

Nadia Tuéni was a Lebanese poet who came to literature to mourn the premature death of her daughter and to sing of her love for her country from the perspective of a woman. She was active in political circles, especially after the June 1967 war. Her husband Ghassan was a representative of the city of Beirut to the Lebanese Parliament, a cabinet minister, and then ambassador of Lebanon to the United Nations. Her works have been published in France mostly by Pierre Seghers, then Jean-Jacques Pauvert and Belfond. She received a prestigious award from the French Academy in 1973 for *Poèmes pour une histoire* (Poems for a Story—published in 1972). In January 1999, a play based on the collection of poems *Juin et les mécréantes* (June and the Miscreants) and inspired by the June 1967 Arab-Israeli war was successfully performed in Paris. Her complete works in French (poetry and prose) were published in Beirut in 1986 by Dar An-Nahar, which has also published three book-length studies of her works. Anthologies of Nadia Tuéni have appeared in Italy and Germany. Although Nadia Tuéni has many readers in Lebanon and the Middle East and has continued to hold the interest of the French public when two posthumous anthologies of her poetry were recently published by major publishing houses (including Flammarion), her reception in the English-speaking world is still largely incomplete. However, *Archives sentimentales d'une guerre au Liban* is all but unknown to the American reading public, despite the fact that some poems from her previous collections have appeared in the *Atlantic Review* and other American journals and that *Liban: Vingt poèmes pour un amour* has been translated into English. I believe, therefore, that this volume might especially appeal to readers of Khalil Gibran, Adonis, Schehadé or Stétié, and more generally to any reader interested in the Middle East or poetry.

Lebanon is the forgotten territory of *la Francophonie*. Its most famous poet, Khalil Gibran, the author of *The Prophet,* has chosen to write in English. Many young Lebanese writers are exiled in Canada, Britain, and the United States. Thus, in a largely trilingual country, the choice of a language—in this case French—is in itself revealing. Languages may divide a country, but they can also create communities beyond the barriers of religion and hatred. French, for Nadia Tuéni, is the language of Rimbaud, Lautréamont, and Surrealist poetry, each of which has had a decisive influence on her work. But she also owes a great debt, on the Arabic side, to the *Shi'r* journal movement, founded in the 1950s by Lebanese avant-garde poets who, like Adonis, were influenced by Surrealism and contributed to what Julia Kristeva would call "a revolution of poetic language" (in *La Révolution du langage poétique*). Influenced by the Surrealistic philosophy and aesthetics of the *Shi'r* movement, Tuéni probably remembered the first Surrealist verses written by Breton and Soupault in *Les Champs Magnétiques,* who used a technique based on random associations and juxtapositions: "ville défaite chevelure" ("city untidy hair"). In this poem, Tuéni is playing on the ambivalence of the adjective *défaite* (untidy) in French: vanquished, destroyed when applied to a city, but merely untidy when applied to hair. Consider the following line as an example of Breton and Soupault's technique: "Suintement cathédrale vertébré supérieur" ("Seeping cathedral vertebrate superior"). In the following lines, Tuéni recalls the postwar absurdist stance of her predecessors: "So in the heat of the sun / I die of incoherence / in bursts." If we come back to the 1956 concepts fundamental to the *Shi'r* movement, as explained in Adonis' *Introduction à la poétique arabe* (Paris: Sindbad, 1985) and translated as *An Introduction to Arab Poetics* (Austin: Univ. of Texas Press, 1990), we learn that the task of the poetic image is to reveal "the ambiguous and the obscure." The word poetry *(shi'r)* originally came from the verb *sha'hara,* "to know," but today this verb means "to feel," and the poet is no longer the one who exclusively knows the truth or has a prophetic role—this role is reserved in Islam for the *'alem.* However, within poetry are remnants of a prophetic dimension, which can be seen carefully expressed in Tuéni's poems—thus, the prophetic claim in the following line: "In my basket these prophecies." This prophetic stance also appears in a poem found after her death among her notes and in which she delineates a new frontier for women (the French original is included here because it is not found in the present volume's selections):

> Femme, j'inventerai pour toi autre chose, un autre langage, un
>   monde, une autre voie.
> Femme, je retrouverai, dessous les sables dormants, ta voie.
> Femme, ce monde n'est pas tien, tu y es étrangère et pourtant tu
>   essaies avec tant de grâce de t'y faire.
> Femme que ton monde soit.

> Woman, for you I will invent something else, another language, a
>   world, another way.
> Woman, I will find, beneath the sleeping sands, your way.
> Woman, this world is not yours, you are a stranger here and
>   nonetheless you try to adapt to it with so much grace.
> Woman may your world be.

The future tense used in this poem—originally published in the posthumous collection of notes titled *Au-delà du regard* (Beyond Sight) and inserted in the second volume of her complete works, *La Prose* (242)—portends a world in which women would not be exiled in a land they cannot control. For a time, it seems that women in this poem are going to be depicted as no more than graceful skaters performing on ice, but the poetic act as genesis is suddenly placed at the center of things. Word, meter, typography (all four lines begin with an uppercase *F* and the word "Femme," while the shorter lines 2 and 4 echo each other), various linguistic elements including a play on tenses (future/present) and moods, a play in use of adjectives and pronouns designating the woman and her double, the woman poet ("Je"/"toi"/"je"/"ta"/"tien"/"tu"/"te"), and a play on determination and gender ("un"/"ton"; "monde" versus "femme"/"voie"/"grâce")—all of this figurative language used in the poem sings of women and their liberation from alienation while telling of the quest for a new poetic language and a new world that the poet vows to invent for all women including herself. *Fiat lux:* this world is created and given to women (it is now their world, as the possessive adjective "ton" indicates). Rather than simply being prophetic (that is, beyond aesthetic pleasure), the poetic voice in the last line sounds indeed like that of a demiurge that creates a new world. From this perspective, beyond the importance of hermeticism in Tuéni's poetry, a larger aim exists in what Jad Hatem has called her poetic quest—a quest that can be compared to one presiding over a mystical poetic writing, a quest that is anchored in her Druze beliefs about immortality and reincarnation.

While the somewhat more traditional poems of *Liban: Vingt poèmes pour un amour* are primarily concerned with Lebanon's symbolic geography, Nadia Tuéni's poetry merges in the second collection with her country's history, especially its history of suffering. The selected poems of *Archives sentimentales d'une guerre an Liban* describe this suffering. The memories of an abandoned garden recede and are replaced by a vision of torture and rotten corpses. The epic gives way to the elegiac. Finally, the reader is invited to reflect on the mimesis of identity: identity of a country, identity of a woman, each one echoing the other. Catharsis and the drama of forgiveness have the last word.

More than twenty years after their first publication in French, many questions raised by these poems remain unanswered. The political situation is still unstable fifteen years after the end of the war and the Taef agreements, which put an end to violence and severe constitutional crises—and several years after the end of the Israeli occupation of southern Lebanon, which first began when these poems were being written. Only a few years ago, the Beit-eddine palace in the Shuf mountains, see of Lebanon's princes in the nineteenth century, was finally returned to the state by the Druze faction. Nadia Tuéni was a member of the Druze religious community (originally born out of a heterodox Shiite Islamic sect) but was married to an Orthodox Christian, and her verse—in which "beats the pulse" *(Oeuvres poétiques complètes,* 321) of the Shuf mountains, ancestral home of the Druze people—modulates to the rhythms of Beirut below. In *Liban: Vingt poèmes pour un amour,* four poems are set specifically in Druze locales ("Le Chôuf," "Deir-el-Kamar," "Beit-eddine," "Jisr-el-Qadi"). The Druze believe that there are a limited number of souls and that each dying Druze immediately gives its soul to another Druze, in a cycle of repeated reincarnations. It is only after several reincarnations that the soul will be judged at the end of time. This belief in the transmigration of souls makes death and life appear as never-ending processes so that a being, and by extension a land in Tuéni's poems, may never die. The overarching theme of unity that prevails in the poems reflects the Druze reference to a strict monotheism. The Druze believe in absolute monotheism and in the direct relationship between one's soul and God. God is the active intellect, the supreme cosmic intellect, and God's prophets are illuminated by this intellect. This sense of unity translates into the social and political landscape.

Religious themes and metaphors, many of them finding their sources in Tuéni's dual Druze and Christian background, are woven into Tuéni's poems on the civil war. Her mother Marguerite Malaquin was a French Christian, while her father Mohammed Ali Hamadé, a diplomat and a writer, was a Druze. Although Tuéni was a secular, modern woman, her interest in metaphysics stems from her Druze upbringing, among other sources. Some factors may help to understand the Druze undercurrents in Tuéni's poetry. First, Tuéni's hermeticism may be influenced by that aspect of Druze religion where knowledge of some symbols is a privilege extended to the enlightened or initiated, allowing them to understand fully the Druze holy books. The Druze also consider Hermes as one of their prophets. Second, and more importantly, the fact that the Druze religion is based on the principles of oneness, equality, social justice, respect for truth, and an aversion for fundamentalism may be one of the reasons for Tuéni's attraction to these same values. Her quest for truth may have its basis in the Druze belief that lying is one of its main taboos. She wrote articles on the Druze religion and customs in newspapers; these articles were reprinted in 1986 in her complete prose works, and we can see some relevant similarities from her Druze experience in the poems, especially her opposition to any fundamentalism. Third, Tuéni notes that traditional Druze poetry excludes love songs and only includes songs for the love of God and country—precisely what she was doing in these two collections of poems. Fourth, as we have seen earlier, the Druze believe in reincarnation, and Tuéni writes prophetically: "I survive my own ashes, and know from memory the future of my time." Fifth, and most importantly, Tuéni writes that in Druze religion, the soul, a feminine element, is fecundated by reason and gives birth to word and time. The religious process of fecundation of the soul by reason is contrasted, particularly in *Archives sentimentales d'une guerre au Liban,* with the brutal (and mostly masculine) madness of a war that largely appears as a rape of the soul. The feminine concept of the soul, expressed through images of the moon as the "night sun" (and analyzed by Jad Hatem in the present volume), also helps the reader to understand Tuéni's identification with her land; in the following poem, the moon appears as a night impregnated by the sun, as a country fertilized by the reason of the poet:

> The wind and its allies
> open themselves just like a woman.
> And all speaks of all.
> The sounds I imagine are rivers or sobs.
> Oh night sun as free as death,
> as that instant when each observes the other.

These aforementioned elements may explain some of the collection's undercurrents. In the last poem, the reference to the freedom of death can be explained by the presence of an omniscient soul that we encounter again in lines of another poem: "I am or am not, depending on the laws of dreams, / but of necessity the seat of

Time. / My heart has looked down upon town and charnel-house [. . .]." Town and charnel-house are one and the same in the last verse and are part of the sustained metaphor of the city as tomb. Metaphorically, Beirut in war becomes a tomb: "listen: the white city is a tomb." Michel de Certeau, in *L'Écriture de l'histoire* (Paris: Gallimard, 1975; translated as *The Writing of History,* New York: Columbia University Press, 1988), compares the writings on history to tombs. As a tomb, writing is a sign of death but also an acknowledgment that death has been integrated into the movement of life. By speaking of death, writing allows for the voices of the dead to continue to be heard. The writing process also has a therapeutic and cathartic function, as it makes it easier for the living to deal with the fact of death and better separate the past from the present. Just as writing was first a way of mourning her lost child, writing history became Tuéni's way of mourning a burning Beirut, metamorphosed into a suffering and mythical woman: "I like / these ashes and their taste of vanished city / more of a city than Antioch and even Babylon." The descriptive system formed in these verses by the loci (Beirut, Antioch and Babylon as vanished cities) is an example of a "literary" category of the memorable. As they are inserted in the poem, the loci are *texts* to remember, insofar as they are variants of a topos that each and every reader is able to reconstitute. According to the Romantic aesthetic used here by the poet, they become a palimpsest: under the surface (Beirut) lies another text (Babylon, Antioch) that the reader, with all his knowledge of the classical literature and history, can easily recognize. This representation of Beirut as—once again—a virtual tomb leads us to acknowledge the importance of the *memento mori* motif at work in the description of these literary locales. As the poet acts here as pilgrim and mourner, she writes for a "non-living thing" (style, city, country) which helps her to live.

Concerning religion, an important way to distance oneself from both the superficial modernity and the reality of the current events is to create another imaginary time, a future that is not necessarily a historical one but rather a prophetic one, or rather a projection in which, beyond death, the unity of the country and the poet is reaffirmed: "Soon earth stopped in her flight / will open itself up like a pomegranate / to the suns of space." In these lines of poetry, images are the basis for a new type of poetic memory, in which the mnemonic role of the commonplace is challenged by a series of images detached from their original narrative and/or ideological motivation and organized into networks of sustained metaphors—or rather here metonymies (earth / pomegranate / grenade / sun). Rather than having a decorative purpose while participating in a cyclical, nonlinear, and paradigmatic network, images are also used to challenge the teleological time that is traditionally associated with the writing of history, a field dominated by men. Images are what help signify an imaginary time in the poems. This imaginary time does not refer to a specific religion and is something quite expected from a modern secular woman like Tuéni, who is aware that religion divides her country and may lead to sectionalism. However, consistent with pre-1975 works by Tuéni is an interest in metaphysics that goes beyond established religions. While Tuéni's poetry is not, as history is, a closed discourse in the third person, it combines, as history does for de Certeau and as religion does as well, the "thinkable" and the origin. She uses the images and the themes rather than the canonical code of religion, which explains why her reference to an imaginary time cannot be reappropriated by men's mastery in a religious context: "Women of my country, / . . . [you] make men believe they are men / . . . even in chaos you discover what endures." In this poem from *Liban: Vingt poèmes pour un amour*, Tuéni makes clear that Lebanese women are effectively the foundation of all that is to last. Hatem rightly claims that the stone in Tuéni's poetry is an image of what will last, an image we find elsewhere in one of the most famous of her poems, also from *Liban: Vingt poèmes pour un amour*, "My Country": "My country, may your stones be for eternity." Ahmad Beydoun, in *Le Liban: Itinéraires dans une guerre incivile* (Lebanon: Itineraries in an

Uncivil War), notes that often historians disqualify historical time and search for eternity or for what Arabic calls *dahr* (indeterminate time). This imaginary time is constructed in the poems through a tale of origins, a primitive scene, in short a reference to an imaginary period of beginnings. *Archives sentimentales d'une guerre au Liban* as Zahida Darwiche Jabbour notes in her book on Nadia Tuéni, is built upon two paradigmatic oppositions: a spatial one between interiority and exteriority but also a temporal one between a paradisaical past and a catastrophic present in which the cultural community is not at peace with itself. The consul's garden of the first part of the collection finally metamorphoses into a fortress. As Jabbour observes, Tuéni builds through a memory, which is both "attic and garden," an atemporal truth grounded in an imaginary previous life. Childhood memories are opposed to images of the sun, sterility, and violent winds that frequently recur in the second part of *Archives sentimentales d'une guerre au Liban* and structure its diverse constituents.

The structure of *Archives sentimentales d'une guerre au Liban* participates in the construction of an imaginary time. While we should note that the same elements return throughout the collection, thus discouraging the critic from studying its three parts separately, the only certainty is that the first part—"Le jardin du consul" (The Consul's Garden), subtitled "hier" ("yesterday")—contains some autobiographical elements and at times refers to the collective memories of a land at peace. It is worth noting that this first part of the collection is an aborted autobiographical novel and tells the stories of real persons, events, or places, such as Tuéni's childhood residence on Kantari Street in Beirut. Expressions borrowed from everyday language reflect an underlying prose style. The lost paradise is that of childhood and, through the figure of the consul, may also refer to colonial Lebanon under the French mandate, or even to the nineteenth-century periods of relative prosperity. The internally perceived details—flowers in the garden, children's costumes—become the starting point of the *rememoratio* process.

However, as Jabbour shows, in this first part of the collection, the consul's ball becomes a mere madman's dance: memory is weaving a palimpsest where certain images almost erase others. It is as if, in this representation, the act of forgetting—celebrated by Ernest Renan as essential to the birth of a nation—was itself a means of selecting elements important to a literary experience. The collection then begins with memory and origin. The vagueness of the preposition "ensuite" ("later"), the subtitle for the second part, titled "folle terre" ("foolish land"), participates in a mythical, imaginary time, one that cements together the first and third parts, while the foolish land is not owned by anyone, as are the garden and the time. The third part, titled "Le futur de mon temps" ("the future of my time") and subtitled "aujourd'hui" ("today"), hesitates between a prophetic future in its title and the present in its subtitle. If the future of the poet's time is today, it may signify that the poems written today, in the urgency of the war's current events, will shed light on the future. At the very least Tuéni is willing to assume a role that no one else wanted: "That is why I have stolen away underneath my tongue a land, / and kept it there like a host." Traditionally, a host is a sign of God's presence; it is also a sign of transubstantiation of the Word and a metaphor for the inspiration process. The image of the host is extremely significant because Lebanon is the force fecundating Tuéni's soul and giving her inspiration. The host is not swallowed but stays protected, under the poet's tongue, as if the poet were defending her land against enemies (Jad Hatem comments upon these lines in his essay)—a role that Tuéni assumed at a critical moment, not only for her country but also for herself, dying from cancer. In sum, Tuéni's cultural and religious background illuminates how she writes about the war and explains how she represents the *universalizing* type of a multicultural Lebanese citizen who is able to go beyond the particularities of the various communities. In this context, we will now try to assess what it means for Nadia Tuéni, an upper-class Druze woman, to write at a time when both she and her nation were experiencing death.

In order to better understand the significance of both collections' publication dates (1979 and 1982), one should remember the context of the Lebanese conflict of 1975 to 1989. The war resulted in part from tensions between various communities (Lebanon has seventeen religious denominations) and from demographic changes that weakened the balance of power. Modern Lebanon has been divided between a largely Maronite Christian view that looks more towards the Mediterranean and the West and a largely Muslim view that assumes an Arab identity. The smaller Christian sects (Greek Catholics and Greek Orthodox) and the Druze do not necessarily share the outlook of Maronites or Muslims, thus complicating the question of Lebanese identity. The Lebanese political system is designed to create a *modus vivendi* among the various communities and identities by distributing power along religious lines, but also by acknowledging religious divisions contributing to the tensions that it is supposed to alleviate. Lebanon's heterogeneity alone does not explain why the political system disintegrated in 1975. One must also reckon with the involvement of external forces that used Lebanon as a battlefield for regional conflicts and cold war rivalry. A roster of those forces includes Syria, Israel, Iran, Saudi Arabia, the two superpowers, and the Palestinian Liberation Organization (PLO). Nadia Tuéni's husband, Ghassan Tuéni, wrote a book titled *Une guerre pour les autres* (A War for the Others) that argues for the primacy of external forces in causing the war.

The first stage of the Lebanese conflict lasted from April 1975 until October 1976. It began with fighting between the Maronite and the Palestinian militias, and when the Lebanese army started to intervene, it soon dissolved along religious lines. Then in 1976, Syrian troops entered Lebanon under the pretext of protecting the population, and Beirut was divided between East (mostly Christian) and West (mostly Muslim). The rest of the country was divided between communal and political factions, creating de facto statelets. Israel then invaded southern Lebanon in 1978 and soon occupied a narrow strip of land along its border, an action condemned by the

United Nations. Soon after, in 1979, *Liban: Vingt poèmes pour un amour* appeared. In it, a poem like "Sud" ("South") appears to be a direct reaction to the historical events taking place. By early 1982, Syria controlled more than half of Lebanese territory, and the mainly Maronite Lebanese Front had created its own ministate around Jounieh, north of Beirut. The Israeli invasion, after a relative period of calm in 1981, marked the high point in the war. The operation "Peace for Galilee," under Israeli Minister of Defense General Sharon, was supposed to stop forty kilometers north of the border according to the plan approved by the Israeli cabinet. But Sharon always intended to advance north in a kind of blitzkrieg that ended with the siege of Beirut. The battle of Beirut then followed and ended with the evacuation of PLO fighters. Then the Israeli army withdrew to Southern Lebanon.

Archives sentimentales d'une guerre au Liban was published in 1982 at the time of the Israeli invasion (June 6, 1982). Nadia Tuéni had been in New York since 1977 with her husband who was Lebanon's representative at the United Nations and who was directly engaged in negotiating peace and the restoration of Lebanon's sovereignty and unity. Yet both were frequently visiting Lebanon and subjected to a life of stress and tragedy. *Archives sentimentales d'une guerre au Liban* was also the last collection published while Tuéni was alive, before she died from cancer in 1983. Thus, she was a witness to the war's worst period, a particularly challenging time for her and for the nation. Some characteristics of the war may help the reader to understand both Tuéni's position and the reaction to her poetry. First, one of the most important consequences of the war was the displacement of persons who became refugees in their own country with little possibility of return. This also caused the displacement of the identities within the nation. Second, the end of the war in 1989 did not resolve the political problems that had caused it; the Arab-Israeli conflict, Lebanese political tensions, and economic problems persisted. The literature produced during the war addressed problems that remained in the postwar era. Third, and most importantly, from a writer's point of view, war produced its own coded discourse. Propaganda was everywhere, and as Tuéni writes, it was easy to "[take] the mountain for the sea." War, then, was also fought with empty words, or words that changed meaning when used by opposing groups and factions. They were used to rewrite history, in particular, in order to adapt it to the needs of the different factions and their conflicting ideologies.

In this context, writing by women has traditionally emphasized the need for a movement that could rid itself of ideological codes. In the case of a Middle Eastern woman writer, the issues associated with gender and history are complicated, as so many critics have observed, because of the cross-cultural context and the complexities of highly coded environments. As the familiar image of the sniper and/or paramilitary militant was forging a new ideal of masculinity, women were, not surprisingly, becoming valued for their essential role as peacekeeper—and also as the fighters' mothers. While some became engaged with the militias, others chose to internalize the conflict and its violence by writing on the war, thus renewing woman writing in Lebanon by reformulating and criticizing the pervasive masculine discourse about the war through the exploration of feminine experiences. This experience may be why women, often less concerned with ideology than with everyday life problems, emerged as a force to testify about the violence of war. This war was not theirs. Women by and large were not actors in politics and the decision-making process; they rather reacted against it. The Lebanese Council of Women protested against violence. Among many events, a sit-in by one hundred women at the American University of Beirut took place in August 1982. Lebanese women writers, such as those Miriam Cooke baptized the "Decentrists," used their literary abilities to counter the male-dominated discourse on war. Their position, as generally acknowledged by critics, profoundly differed from the ideological use of language during the war. One of the first poems of *Archives sentimentales d'une guerre au Liban* addresses a way to alter or eliminate meaning and

communication by describing the well-known funerary portraits of
the dead fighters and opposing word and image:

> *How sad it is that often times*
> *the image cuts short the word.* [. . .]

> Those who have died are entitled,
> to a great black portrait
> upon a blank wall [. . .]

In danger of being dominated as a woman poet in a predomi-
nantly male environment and concerned with the predominantly
male discourse about war, Tuéni had to find a way beyond the vio-
lent superimposed manifestations of a canonical modernity. How
does this happen in the two collections? A highly coded and perva-
sive trope (country/woman) "reads" and allegorizes the war. The
country becomes for the poet a pregnant mother: "the mighty earth
holds me in her organs." In this context, memory is but an umbili-
cal cord—"Memories take the form of an umbilical cord, attached
to every face." Nadia Tuéni is not the only woman writer to play on
this contiguity and, moreover, to play on the symbolic position of
the masculine and the feminine in what could be considered as a
"sexual difference" framework. However, in her work, the poet's
body is a sustained metaphor for the country, as sexual images are
produced and explained by the historical events at play: "oh this hate
that fecundates the earth, / like a woman's warm blood." In associ-
ating, as Jabbour notes, hate with the menstrual blood, Tuéni
engages in a kind of woman writing deriving from the woman's
body, as is also the case in the following instance: "Now, let me go /
for I capsize from the other side of my womb / red with the blood
of all." In so doing, like Hélène Cixous, she emphasizes the role
of the mother's body in shaping the adult self and its behavior, thus
reacting against the traditional patriarchal stands. Tuéni's poetry
could appear as an appropriate response to the male domination

symbolized by the celebration of masculinity in the historical context.

How does this response lead to a rewriting of history in which unity along with identification are the main themes? How do poetry editions replace the masculine linear narratives of nationhood? Michel de Certeau sees the writing of history as a resurrection of the past, as the incessant rebuilding of a mythical origin that can never be totally reappropriated. What cannot be forgotten (the dead city, the dead child) functions then in Tuéni's poetry as an interpretant of the poems and points to their significance. The dialectical mechanism of presupposition rooted in forgetfulness involves both the state of forgetfulness and its transformation into a vehicle of interpretation through the perception of the implicit, present in absentia in the text. Thus, because the memorable landscape of the country also functions in the poems as a trope, the conditions for an aesthetic contemplation by the reader perceiving this implicit metamorphosis (landscape/trope) are reinforced, as is evident in these lines from two poems of *Archives sentimentales d'une guerre au Liban*:

> "[. . .] All things possess such beauty only because all will die,
> in an instant."

> The land has died of beauty,
> killed by a burst of laughter.
> A bombshell in the ground has hollowed out a smile.

Here, Tuéni's relation to death informs her writing in a way in which the title of *Archives sentimentales d'une guerre au Liban* is completely justified. "Archives," wrote de Certeau, reduce the world to a set of categories that facilitates its understanding. As an archivist, Tuéni researches correspondences in the history of the Lebanese civil war. But as a poet, she builds synesthetic correspondences between the elements of contemporary life. In her writing, the resurrection of the past—and this is particularly true of *Liban: Vingt poèmes pour un amour*—is placed on the same level as the power of aesthetic emotion conveyed by artistic forms. Beauty becomes a means of verisimilitude and liveliness. This relationship is achieved in two ways: on the one hand, an aesthetic emotion comes from the powerful presence of forms, and on the other hand, a resurrection of the past conveys the verisimilitude of these *historical* collections of poems. This resurrection of the past suggests the rewriting of history to echo, analyze, and express the crises of identity described earlier, and it is found in the poems when Tuéni incorporates isolated elements of the ideological discourse: " 'Fierce combat'. / 'New mediations'. / 'Factions concerned.' " The surprising expressions in the poem's idiolect, such as clichés of propaganda or other examples imported from the sociolect, have to be incorporated in the poetry in order to cancel out the prosaic reality of the present war and that of the words commonly used to describe the war. Using this approach, the poet is able to elaborate and project a vision *beyond* the violent discourses associated with war. Nowhere is this process more visible than in the following poem:

> Ancient land,
> vital memory of these mutilated bodies
> that legitimize you.
> History stands erect upon your shores,
> while my mountain's pulse beats.

Beirut remains in many respects what Tuéni has described as a "city heated white hot by the word." Jabbour rightly observes that as the warrior "cannot hear the scratch of the poet's pen," the sterile "closed discourse" is opposed to the poetic word. As explained above, a way of distancing oneself from this closed discourse is to incorporate it into poems. And as Jabbour observes, the war vocabulary is inserted in the poems: to "kill," "shoot," "bombshell," and so forth. War gives birth to words, as night begets day: "[we] uttered the words that kill." Accordingly, Tuéni is constructing alternative forms of expression to the dominant ideology through a systematic attack on clichés and, in Mallarmean terms, gives meaning back to the words of the tribe, as in the following verses:

AN IDEA IS SHOT AND A MAN DROPS DEAD.
Always scarlet red the power of words,
more murderous than a gesture.
Those who live in the sunlight of the word,
upon the runaway horse of slogans,
those,
shatter the windows of the universe.

The very negativity that characterizes *topoi* in the poet's discourse leads to a liberation of images from the prevailing influence of *topoi*. As *topoi* become mere citations in the text, they are replaced by images that construct textual memory. As Jabbour rightly observes, Tuéni also uses here and elsewhere the graphic and rhythmic dimension of the poem to transform words into ammunition:"One has to understand that laughter is but an illusion, / exactly-between-the-creator-and-the created."

What are the other means that poetry uses to separate itself from the misuse (or abuse) of language? Ahmad Beydoun asserts that as a consequence of war's ossified ideological language, poetry tends to evolve into a more hermetic form *(Le Liban: Itinéraires dans une guerre incivile,* 72). Thus, it is no coincidence that in a lecture included in her complete prose works, Tuéni writes that she is looking for the real as a projection of human mystery, not the kind of "real" perceived by the senses. Incidentally, she also sees hermeticism as a means of canceling out the sexual difference at play between male and female roles in her writing. For Tuéni, Andrée Chedid, a well-known French woman writer born in Cairo into a Lebanese family and author of numerous works, including *Terre et poésie,* is an inspiration, as she introduced hermeticism and a sense of duration and death to a generation of poets.

In Tuéni's literary career, Chedid played an even more important role, by helping her to formulate the relation between poetry and land. In 1969, after the shock of the 1967 war, Tuéni spoke about an earlier lecture by Chedid in Beirut. According to Tuéni, in a lecture published in her complete prose works, Chedid said that poetry and land are both an integral part of that which defines human beings, that the very origin of the noun *versus* (related to the verb *verto*) first meant "furrow" and that Tuéni's "poetic land" is a "fully inhabited land." Tuéni proceeds to say that her "poetic land" ("terre poétique") had been revealed to her through the 1967 war. From her perspective, the awareness of one's particular land implies a particular vision of the world that includes a mountainous hinterland *(arrière-pays)*, an imaginary desert, and a corporeal relationship to her country. The *arrière-pays* here, in the same way the term was used in poet Yves Bonnefoy's eponymous book, is a translation of her own imaginary identity and an internalization of a pre-symbolic universe that serves to cancel out the reality of historical time. Indeed, in *Liban: Vingt poèmes pour un amour,* landscape and language are intertwined to a point reminiscent of Fouad Gabriel Naffah's *La description de l'homme, du cadre et de la lyre.* Both Tuéni and Naffah insist on the importance of one's harmony with the landscape. Naffah was a close friend of both Nadia and her husband Ghassan and was published by Dar An-Nahar, which the Tuénis own.

As Tuéni's individual quest becomes a collective one, it seems that her voice is replaced by that of her country. Tuéni's starting point is to acknowledge the cell-like proliferation of the madness that war represents for her in order to condemn it. At the beginning of the eighties, war was indeed bordering on madness. *Archives sentimentales d'une guerre au Liban* begins with the depiction of a dead body, cut in half, and continues with images of bloody rain, tears, and bullets. Hatem is right to point out that madness is one of the structuring elements of Tuéni's collection. It may take the form of a schizophrenic divide between land and country, between one citizen and another, but also a divide within those individuals whose reasoning is diminished or obscured. The last poem of this collection, dedicated to Tuéni's husband, speaks about the noise of madness's peal. Tuéni writes that even storytellers have nothing to say, as "[four] suns stand guard lest / time invent a story." In this context the poet's first task is to listen in order to construct a meaning: "I lower my voice to better hear / the Country howl." The context of Tuéni's poems is thus that of a crisis both in time and in space, and writing is born out of this complex crisis, as the poet asks herself countless questions about her identity and denies war the power to shape that identity. The following poem, appearing at the end of *Archives sentimentales d'une guerre au Liban,* addresses this crisis and the search for identity, and it tackles this challenge in terms that are relevant not only for the poet but also for divided Beirut and all Lebanese citizens. In this poem the use of the French neutral masculine *(né,* instead of *née* for "born," *présent* instead of *présente* "present," both referring to a general role, situation, or persona rather than to a simple and convenient mask) is the tool that Tuéni uses to make the reader aware that the poetic voice that utters "I" belongs to all Lebanese people:

Was I born of a lie
in a country that did not exist?

Am I one tribe at the confluence of two opposing bloods?

But perhaps I am not.
[. . .]
Who will make me real?

Here again, division and the longing for unity organize what has become a collective rather than individual quest, in which "I" in the previous poem could represent the Lebanese identity. As the collection unfolds, the reassuring preliminary autobiographical references to childhood and to a coherent and/or historical time no longer seem to hold. What will actualize identity as it seems to be reduced to a mere potentiality? Writing seems to be the appropriate answer. This may be why the collection relentlessly celebrates the poetic word. One thing is clear though: in postwar Lebanon, readers have found in Tuéni a powerful symbol of their nation's identity and a rallying voice for women. And this is the case for three main reasons: a concern for gender that leads her to rewrite Lebanese history from the point of view of the suffering and the oppressed; a longing for unity that, beyond the influence of feminism, comes not only from an almost corporeal attachment to, and identification with, her land but also from her Druze upbringing; and finally, an incessant effort to make out of language a testimony and a spiritual act. She did not write about the everyday difficulties associated with war like some of her counterparts. Rather, she chose to create a new poetic language that captured the fragile essence of her troubled country and exposed the many crises of identities present in the war. By identifying with her country, she placed herself beyond all parties and created a sacred river that irrigates her poems.

The present volume includes forty poems, followed by two short essays, a biographical profile on Tuéni, and a short bibliography. It is this editor's hope that these two essays will facilitate the understanding of the poems from *Archives sentimentales d'une guerre au Liban,* generally considered more difficult to access and understand. The translations have been made by Samuel Hazo, professor emeritus at Duquesne University, and Paul B. Kelley, a contemporary French and Francophone literature specialist who taught at Wake Forest University and recently collaborated on a translation of Deleuze. I am grateful to Samuel Hazo for allowing me to include his translation of *Liban: Vingt Poèmes pour un amour (Lebanon: Twenty Poems for One Love),* first published in English by Byblos Press in 1990 in New York. The reader may appreciate how this earlier collection, which first appeared in French in 1979, facilitates the understanding of *Archives sentimentales d'une guerre au Liban* and anticipates several important themes of the 1982 collection. Professor Syrine Hout, from the American University of Beirut, has contributed an essay titled "Home, Politics, and Exile" on Nadia Tuéni's *Archives sentimentales d'une guerre au Liban,* in which she addresses the mingling of personal, national, and regional issues affecting

Lebanon and the region when the poems were written. Jad Hatem, professor and former chair of philosophy at Saint-Joseph University, who is himself a celebrated poet and the editor of Tuéni's complete works in French, has contributed an essay titled "The Night Sun." Hatem has chosen to analyze one of the poems from *Archives sentimentales d'une guerre au Liban* and focuses his attention on the spiritual aspects of Tuéni's poetry.

This book would not have appeared without the work of Ghassan Tuéni, the Dar An-Nahar Group, and the Nadia Tuéni Foundation. Nor would it have appeared without the support and dedication of Mary Selden Evans, John Fruehwirth, Amy Barone, and the rest of the staff at Syracuse University Press. I would also like to thank the dean of Amherst College for a grant that helped to complete this volume and the French Cultural Mission in Lebanon for its support. In the United States, I am deeply indebted to my friends and colleagues at the University of the Pacific, as well as to Paul Kelley and David Commins, for their invaluable help on earlier drafts of my introduction. Parts of an earlier draft of this introduction have been presented as conference papers delivered at the 2001 Modern Language Association convention and the 2002 International Colloquium in 20th- and 21st-Century French Studies at the University of Connecticut at Hartford. In Lebanon, numerous friends at the American University of Beirut, Saint-Joseph University, the Oriental Library and elsewhere have greatly facilitated my work. I am particularly indebted to Najla Chéhab, Farès Sassine, and the entire Dar An-Nahar staff. I would also like to acknowledge the help of the Smayra and Harmouche families and express my gratitude to Jacqueline, Raffoul, and Michel Smayra for their generous hospitality these last few years. I particularly want to thank Liliane Smayra and Alexandre Harmouche for guiding me through Beirut's streets and Lebanon's mountains. Last but not least, I would like to thank Adnan Haydar and Michael Beard for generously accepting my manuscript for their fine series Middle East Literature in Translation. I can only hope that this bilingual edition will contribute to the natural westward growth of a reading public for Middle Eastern Francophone literature, at a time when the most favorable conditions are present for a renaissance in Lebanese literature.

Although a comprehensive knowledge of Lebanon, Lebanese contemporary literature, and the Lebanese conflict may shed light on the selected poems, Nadia Tuéni addresses themes and topics that are largely universal and, thus, will be appreciated far beyond Lebanese borders. Some of these themes include violence, loss, reconciliation, and hope. Above all, the reader will witness her love for her land, its history and its people, and may reflect on the spiritual dimension found in these poems. Nowhere is this spiritual dimension more apparent than in her testament piece from 1982 that first appeared in *Oeuvres complètes: La Prose,* page 253. I supply below an English translation by Ghassan Tuéni of passages from this work:

J'ai décidé de consigner à partir d'aujourd'hui 25 avril 1982 les petits faits de ma vie de cancéreuse bien soignée.

Il y a quelque chose de fascinant dans cette folie cellulaire, dans ce désordre mortel, qui tient en échec la médicine.

J'ai tendance à croire que l'ordre de se révolter contre l'harmonie vivante, est donné de quelque part au fond de moi, par mon vrai moi, et pour des raisons que j'ignore, mais qui doivent porter en elles une sagesse certaine.

J'appartiens à un pays qui chaque jour se suicide tandis qu'on l'assassine. En fait, j'appartiens à un pays plusieurs fois mort. Pourquoi ne mourrais-pas moi aussi de cette mort rongeante et laide, lente et vicieuse, de cette mort libanaise?

J'ai dit un jour que je ressemblais à ma Folle Terre : elle et moi expions un crime de double identité.

As of today 25 April 1982 I have decided to register the little facts of my life as a well-treated cancer-patient.

There is something fascinating in this cellular folly, in this mortal disorder that medicine cannot vanquish.

I tend to believe that the order to revolt against the harmony of life emanates from somewhere in my deepest inner self, by my true self, for reasons that I ignore, but which should bear some certain wisdom unknown, yet real.

I belong to a country that commits suicide every day, while it is being assassinated. As a matter of fact, I belong to a country that died several times. Why should I not die too of this gnawing, ugly, slow, and vicious death, of this Lebanese death?

I have written once that I resemble my Foolish Land: we are both expiating a crime of double identity.

Lebanon

Twenty Poems for One Love

Liban

Vingt poèmes pour un amour

Translated by Samuel Hazo

A Nayla,

à ceux qui furent ses amis,

aux enfants de mon pays.

To Nayla,

To those who were their friends,

To the children of my country.

Prologue

C'est déjà l'Orient,
où le blanc domine,
où le jaune, l'ocre et le rose,
ont élu royal domicile,
où l'arbre est unique,
la folie solitaire,
où l'homme repense la pensée . . .

Prologue

This is already the Orient,
where white peaks have dominion,
where yellow, rose and ochre
have made their royal residence,
where every tree is itself
and madness isolated,
where man rethinks thought.

Mon pays

Mon pays longiligne a des bras de prophète.
Mon pays que limitent la haine et le soleil.
Mon pays où la mer a des pièges d'orfèvre,
que l'on dit villes sous-marines,
que l'on dit miracle ou jardin.
Mon pays où la vie est un pays lointain.
Mon pays est mémoire
d'hommes durs comme la faim,
et de guerres plus anciennes
que les eaux du Jourdain.

Mon pays qui s'éveille,
projette son visage sur le blanc de la terre.
Mon pays vulnérable est un oiseau de lune.
Mon pays empalé sur le fer des consciences.
Mon pays en couleurs est un grand cerf-volant.
Mon pays où les vents sont un nœud de vipères.
Mon pays qui d'un trait refait le paysage.

Mon pays qui s'habille d'uniformes et de gestes,
qui accuse une fleur coupable d'être fleur.
Mon pays au regard de prière et de doute.
Mon pays où l'on meurt quand on en a le temps.
Mon pays où la loi est un soldat de plomb.
Mon pays qui me dit: "Prenez-moi au sérieux",
mais qui tourne et s'affole comme un pigeon blessé.
Mon pays difficile tel un très long poème.
Mon pays bien plus doux que l'épaule qu'on aime.
Mon pays qui ressemble à un livre d'enfant,
où le canon dérange la belle-au-bois-dormant.

My Country

My long-limbed country has the arms of a prophet.
My country, whose boundaries are drawn by hatred and the sun,
where the sea possesses goldsmith's traps
called sunken cities or miracles or gardens . . .
My country, where life is remote as a foreign land . . .
My country's a memory
of men hard as hunger,
and of wars more ancient
than the waters of the Jordan.

My awakening country
casts a shadow of its face on the land's whiteness.
My country is vulnerable as a bird from the moon.
My country impales itself on the sword of conscience.
My country is a giant kite of many colors.
My country's winds are a knot of vipers.
My country with one stroke remakes its geography.

My country, costumed in uniforms and mere gestures,
condemns a flower for being a flower.
My country has a look of holiness and doubt.
My country is where men die when they have time for it.
My country's law is a toy soldier.
My country begs me, "Take me seriously,"
then turns and goes berserk as a wounded pigeon.
My country is difficult as a long poem.
My country is softer than a lover's shoulder.
My country's like a child's storybook
where the theme awakens Sleeping Beauty.

Mon pays de montagnes que chaque bruit étonne.
Mon pays qui ne dure que parce qu'il faut durer.
Mon pays tu ressembles aux étoiles filantes,
qui traversent la nuit sans jamais prévenir.
Mon pays mon visage,
la haine et puis l'amour
naissent à la façon dont on se tend la main.
Mon pays que ta pierre soit une éternité.
Mon pays mais ton ciel est un espace vide.

Mon pays que le choix ronge comme une attente.
Mon pays que l'on perd un jour sur le chemin.
Mon pays qui se casse comme un morceau de vague.
Mon pays où l'été est un hiver certain.
Mon pays qui voyage entre rêve et matin.

My country's mountains are startled by noise.
My country lasts because it must.
My country is like those shooting stars
that flash across the night without warning.
My country, you are my face
where love and hate are born as easily as a hand is opened.
My country, may your stones be for eternity.
My country, may your heaven be more than mere emptiness.

My country, which decision devours like patience . . .
My country that a traveler loses on the road one day . . .
My country, which is coming asunder like a wave's crest . . .
My country, where summer and winter are the same . . .
My country, you are a journey between dreams and dawn.

Beyrouth

Quelle soit courtisane, érudite, ou dévote,
péninsule des bruits, des couleurs, et de l'or,
ville marchande et rose, voguant comme une flotte,
qui cherche à l'horizon la tendresse d'un port,
elle est mille fois morte, mille fois revécue.
Beyrouth des cent palais, et Béryte des pierres,
où l'on vient de partout ériger ces statues,
qui font prier les hommes, et font hurler les guerres.

Ses femmes aux yeux de plages qui s'allument la nuit,
et ses mendiants semblables à d'anciennes pythies.
A Beyrouth chaque idée habite une maison.
A Beyrouth chaque mot est une ostentation.
A Beyrouth l'on décharge pensées et caravanes,
flibustiers de l'esprit, prêtresses ou bien sultanes.
Qu'elle soit religieuse, ou qu'elle soit sorcière,
ou qu'elle soit les deux, ou qu'elle soit charnière,
du portail de la mer ou des grilles du levant,
qu'elle soit adorée ou qu'elle soit maudite,
qu'elle soit sanguinaire, ou qu'elle soit d'eau bénite,
qu'elle soit innocente, ou qu'elle soit meurtrière,
en étant phénicienne, arabe, ou roturière,
en étant levantine aux multiples vertiges,
comme ces fleurs étranges fragiles sur leurs tiges,
Beyrouth est en orient le dernier sanctuaire,
où l'homme peut toujours s'habiller de lumière.

Beirut

Let her be courtesan, scholar, or saint,
a peninsula of din, of color, and of gold,
a hub of rose sailing like a fleet
which scans the horizon for a harbor's tenderness.
Beirut has died a thousand times and been reborn a thousand
     times.
Beirut of a hundred palaces, Beryte of the stones
where pilgrims from everywhere have raised statues
that make men pray and wars begin.

Her women have eyes like beaches where lights shine by night,
and her beggars are ancient as Pythonesses.
In Beirut each thought inhabits a mansion.
In Beirut each word is a drama.
In Beirut, thoughts deliver filibusters of the mind,
and caravans bear priestesses and sultans' wives.
Let her be nun or sorceress or both,
or let her be the hinge
of the sea's portal or the gateway to the East,
let her be adored or let her be cursed,
let her be thirsty for blood or holy water,
let her be innocent or let her be a murderess.
By being Phoenician, Arabic, or of the people—
Levantine—or of such dizzying variety
as strange and fragile flowers atop stems,
Beirut is the last place in the Orient
where man can dress himself in light.

Byblos

Tranquille comme un juste
ancienne comme la vérité,
Byblos ô mon amour à la couleur ambrée,
des choses que le vent ranime de mémoire en mémoire,
tel un feu domestique lorsque le soir descend.
Et sur le port,
debout contre la mer écartelée
le premier des soleils
évite encore une fois l'écueil de l'horizon,
pour renaître demain vieilli comme la terre.
Byblos ô mon amour s'habille de poussière.
Mais quand la nuit éclaire tous les chemins du temps,
on voit au fond de l'eau,
la dure transparence des mondes qui se cognent.
Byblos ô mon amour a le silence pour haleine.
Ecoute,
c'est le bruit-plein des vaisseaux qui ramènent,
un peu de sable, un océan,
un équateur, un occident.
J'entends brûler midi,
et dans nos yeux soudain plus grands,
l'écriture a jailli.
Byblos ô mon amour,
n'est que le cœur du temps.

Byblos

Calm as a just man,
ancient as truth itself,
my amber and beloved Byblos,
you keep for our remembering
what every wind redeems from memory
like hearthfires that reveal themselves
only with the fall of night.
Descending halved and upright at the sea's horizon
far beyond your port,
the sourcing sun avoids once more at dusk
the reef of distance
to be reborn at dawn complete as the very earth.
Byblos my beloved, you are robed in dust,
but like a road illuminated in the dark
you let us glimpse as through the clearest sea
the hard transparencies of worlds in collision.
Byblos my beloved, you breathe silence,
but your silence lets us hear
the sound of sand, oceans,
the earth's equator and the western world.
Your noons burn before us
until our enlarging eyes
conceive and speak epiphanies.
Byblos my beloved,
you are time's heartbeat.

Tripoli

C'est la ville à trois feuilles,
large comme un sourire;
ni temples ni prières pour faire tourner la terre.
C'est la mer qui découvre un navire,
aussi transparent qu'un oiseau de jour.
Une aube racontée par d'anciens troubadours.
C'est l'oranger qui succède à l'histoire.
L'homme et la mort qui vivent un sablier d'amour.
C'est une forteresse tracée au crayon noir.
Enfin des souks étroits enroulés comme une coiffure,
avec des épingles de sucre,
et des ruelles d'enluminure.
Voilà les filets du matin,
qu'étalent comme une parure,
des pêcheurs fils de Paladins.
Ce sont des minarets qui nous parlent voyage.
Souvent, ici, le temps se trompe de chemin.

Tripoli

This is the city of three leaves.
Wide as a smile,
it offers neither temples nor prayers to make the earth turn.
It is like a sea that reveals a ship
as plainly as the sky accepts a bird.
Ancient troubadours sang at its dawn.
It is where the orange tree inherits history.
Man and death live in an hourglass of love.
Tripoli's a fort outlined in pencil.
The narrow souks roll up like a headdress
secured with pins of spun sugar.
The alleyways dance with color.
Here the fishermen, sons of Paladins,
spread out their nets each morning like fine garments.
Here the minarets speak to us of voyages.
Here time at times takes the wrong road.

Saïda

Sidon l'ensoleillée a planté d'ombre ses fenêtres,
pareilles aux îles du matin.
Ses créneaux coupent en deux la nuit.
Ainsi la mémoire n'a plus d'ailes,
une épave de lune dérive dans ses yeux.
Etrangère Sidon parfumée comme un rite,
à cause de la mer tu es péripétie.
Tu t'en vas simple comme l'hiver,
sur ton dos des traces de terre,
des traces d'encre et de murailles,
des traces d'hommes et de batailles.
Sauvages furent tes tendresses,
ta voix remplie de coquillages.
Un moment, quelque part,
précieuse comme un vieil ivoire,
s'obstine l'ombre des Templiers.
Et parfois dans les plis du vent,
l'haleine épaisse des orangers.

Saïda

Saïda of the sunlight, you have planted shadows in your windows
like islands in the morning.
Your crenellated towers slice the night in half.
Memory has no wings for you.
Flotsam of moonlight swims in your eyes.
Saïda the foreigner, you are anointed like a rite.
Because you face the sea, you are Perepitia.
You vanish easier than winter—
a trace of the earth here or there,
an echo of ink, of walls,
of men, of battles.
You have a savage tenderness.
Your voice is the voice in shells from the sea.
You last like old ivory
from an instant in history—
the shadows of the Templars.
You last in the breath of time,
in the musk of the orange trees.

Tyr

Moi Tyr aux mains liquides,
qui se pose un instant dans la paix de l'oubli.
Moi cette reine de Phénicie que le temps a déshabillée,
et qui marche pieds nus dans l'eau jusqu'aux genoux.
Ainsi glisse en phrases de pourpre,
une histoire bruyante, de mort, de temps, d'amour;
un livre de soleil,
têtu comme l'odeur d'un matin à Carthage.
Une histoire de vaisseaux qui émigrent encore,
et déchirent au passage un morceau de nuit ronde.
Moi Tyr aux mille grains de mer,
que la lumière debout reçoit sur sa terrasse,
lorsque trébuche l'univers.
Moi Tyr où souffle encore un orage de pierres.

Tyre

I, Tyre, whose hands are water,
who stands for a moment in the peace of oblivion . . .
I, that queen of Phoenicia denuded by time,
who wades barelegged in water up to her knees . . .
Thus pass by in secrets of purple
my stark tales of death, of time, of love,
my book of the sun,
enduring like the scent of dawn in Carthage.
I am a history of ships that still depart
and take with them in going
a small piece of the night.
I, Tyre, have received a thousand grains of the sea
like light upon my terraces
each time the universe convulses.
I am Tyre where a storm of stone rages.

En montagne libanaise

Se souvenir—du bruit du clair de lune,
lorsque la nuit d'été se cogne à la montagne,
et que traîne le vent,
dans la bouche rocheuse des Monts Liban.

Se souvenir—d'un village escarpé,
posé comme une larme au bord d'une paupière;
on y rencontre un grenadier,
et des fleurs plus sonores
qu'un clavier.

Se souvenir—de la vigne sous le figuier,
des chênes gercés que Septembre abreuve,
des fontaines et des muletiers,
du soleil dissout dans les eaux du fleuve.

Se souvenir—du basilic et du pommier,
du sirop de mûres et des amandiers.

Alors chaque fille était hirondelle,
ses yeux remuaient comme une nacelle,
sur un bâton de coudrier.

Se souvenir—de l'ermite et du chevrier,
des sentiers qui mènent au bout du nuage,
du chant de l'Islam, des châteaux croisés,
et des cloches folles du mois de Juillet.

In the Lebanese Mountains

Remember—the noise of moonlight
when the summer night collides with a peak
and traps the wind
in the rocky caves of the mountains of Lebanon.

Remember—a town on a sheer cliff
set like a tear on the rim of an eyelid;
one discovers there a pomegranate tree
and rivers more sonorous
than a piano.

Remember—the grapevine under the fig tree,
the cracked oak that September waters,
fountains and muleteers,
the sun dissolving in the river currents.

Remember—basil and apple tree,
mulberry syrup and almond groves.

Each girl was a swallow then
whose eyes moved like a gondola
swung from a hazel branch.

Remember—the hermit and goatherd,
paths that rise to the edge of a cloud,
the chant of Islam, crusaders' castles,
and wild bells ringing through July.

Se souvenir—de chacun, de tous,
du conteur, du mage, et du boulanger,
des mots de la fête, de ceux des orages,
de la mer qui brille comme une médaille,
dans le paysage.

Se souvenir—d'un souvenir d'enfant,
d'un secret royaume qui avait notre âge;
nous ne savions pas lire les présages,
dans ces oiseaux morts au fond de leurs cages,
sur les Monts Liban.

Remember—each one, everyone,
storyteller, prophet and baker,
the words of the feast and the words of the storm,
the sea shining like a medal in the landscape.

Remember—the child's recollection
of a secret kingdom just our age.
We did not know how to read the omens
in those dead birds in the bottoms of their cages,
in the mountains of Lebanon.

Femmes de mon pays

Femmes de mon pays,
une même lumière durcit vos corps,
une même ombre les repose;
doucement élégiaques en vos métamorphoses.
Une même souffrance gerce vos lèvres,
et vos yeux sont sertis par un unique orfèvre.
Vous,
qui rassurez la montagne,
qui faites croire à l'homme qu'il est homme,
à la cendre qu'elle est fertile,
au paysage qu'il est immuable.
Femmes de mon pays,
vous, qui dans le chaos retrouvez le durable.

Women of My Country

Women of my country,
a common light hardens your bodies,
and a common darkness lets them rest
in a soft elegy of change.
A common suffering cracks your lips,
and your eyes have been set by the same unique jeweler.
You reassure mountains,
make men believe they are men
convince ashes of their own fertility
and tell the land that it will never pass away.
Women of my country,
even in chaos you discover what endures.

Le Chôuf

En un point de l'espace,
telles deux mains qui se joignent,
l'homme et la forme se retrouvent,
l'homme et la pierre se ressemblent;
car les aigles choisissent pour poser leur splendeur
les plus hauts sanctuaires.
Ici sur la montagne soleil et vent se frottent,
tout devient silence et couleur.
Le Chôuf est un oiseau grandement solitaire,
avec des voiles blancs et des gestes de mort.

The Shuf

At one point in space,
like two clasped hands,
man and form discover one another,
man and stone resemble one another.
Eagles rest their splendor
in the highest mountains.
Here on these mountains, sun and wind commingle.
Everything becomes silence and color.
The Shuf is a noble solitary bird
with white veils and the gestures of death.

Deir el-Kamar

Ton regard est une prière.
Tu règnes sur la nuit à la saison solaire.
Ame sœur de l'été,
puisqu'à chaque instant tu t'inventes,
le temps n'a plus sa raison d'être.
Un basilic à tes fenêtres,
déjà tu sais que vivre est la pire passion.
Avec un bruit d'église, un jardin de ruelles,
tu traverses l'espace sur la pointe des ailes.
Ainsi dans ta main droite une Princesse brune,
et dans l'autre, une lune.

Deir el-Kamar

Your very look is a prayer.
You rule the night in the age of the sun.
Soul-sister of summer,
since you invent yourself instant by instant,
time no longer has reason to be.
With basil at your every window,
you still know that living is the worst passion of all.
Amid the din of churches and garden-like alleyways,
you suspend space on the points of your wings.
You hold in your right hand a dark-haired princess,
and in your left the moon.

Beit-eddine

Ici poussent la fleur et la géométrie.
Les mots ont une odeur de rose.
Quelques secrets s'envolent où la main nue se pose,
le vent dans les cyprès est un amour ancien.
Beit-eddine épie la vallée
dans la ruse de ses allées.
Les murs ont pleuré de couleurs,
et les plafonds voyagent comme l'eau des fontaines.
Ici dorment matins et violents coups de lune;
quand au bord d'une cour une forme s'affole,
c'est à peine une arcade et déjà un envol,
d'oiseaux que la lumière oublie dans les jardins.

Beit-eddine

Blossoms and patterns grow here.
Words have the scent of roses.
At the touch of a hand some secrets escape,
and the wind in the cypresses remembers a lost love.
From the wiles of its passageways,
Beit-eddine spies on its valley.
Its walls have wept colors,
and its ceilings sway like fountaining water.
Mornings and ruthless moonlight sleep here.
When something swarms in a courtyard's nook,
it seems like an arcade in shadow or a flight
of birds forgotten by light in the gardens.

Jisr el-Qadi

En un lieu de cruches et de vent.
En un lieu de pont et de route.
En un lieu jeune comme l'eau.
En un lieu où le pied se pose
comme une fleur sur un ruisseau.
En un lieu où l'oiseau n'est qu'un bruit sur ta joue.
En un lieu qui ne veut rien dire.
En un lieu qui demeure précis comme une enfance.
En un lieu que les lunes transforment en absence.
En un lieu à deux mains un tour et de l'argile.
En un lieu où l'on peut se taire.
En un lieu où le monde a la forme d'un verre!

Jisr el-Qadi

In a place of wind and clay pitchers,
in a place of a bridge and a road,
in a place as fresh as water,
in a place where a foot touches
softly as a blossom on a stream,
in a place where a bird's passing
is only a pressure by your cheek,
in a place which means nothing,
in a place which stays precise as childhood,
in a place transformed into absence by moons,
in a place of two hands, a potter's wheel and some clay,
in a place where you can be still,
in a place where the world is a glass you drink from.

Hommes de mon pays

Dans nos montagnes il y a des hommes,
ce sont des amis de la nuit;
leurs yeux brillent du noir des chèvres,
leurs gestes raides comme la pluie.
Ils ont pour maître l'olivier,
simple vieillard aux bras croisés.
Eux,
leurs mains sont de chardons,
leurs poitrines sanctuaires,
"le ciel tourne autour de leurs fronts,
comme un insecte lourd à la chaude saison."
Dans nos montagnes il y a des hommes,
qui ressemblent au tonnerre,
et savent que le monde est gros comme une pomme.

Men of My Country

In our mountains are men
who are friends of the night,
whose eyes shine like goats' eyes,
whose gestures are straight as rain.
The olive tree is their master,
these simple old men with arms crossed.
Their hands are thistles.
Their chests are sanctuaries,
and "heaven revolves around their heads
like a plump insect in a hot season."
In our mountains are men
who resemble thunder,
who know that the world is ripe as an apple.

Annâya

En pays de prières
la lumière habite un vitrail.
Le matin glisse dans la chapelle,
un moine et son ombre jumelle.
La vierge dort sous son émail.
Le soleil professe et travaille,
sur les terres de Mâr Charbel.

En pays de prières,
la montagne a un double nez;
des larmes en feuilles de peupliers.
On cultive entre les rochers,
graines et fleurs de chapelets.

En pays de prières
la lune quitte son orbite.
Un enfant cache dans la bruyère,
un Ave plus quatre Pater.

Et la nuit ouvre sa portière,
s'en échappe une Carmélite,
qui serre dans son aumônière,
des dragées blanches d'eau bénite.
La lune quitte son orbite,
pour rejoindre sur la clairière
la robe brune de l'Ermite.

En pays de prières,
les corps sont bribes d'un même secret.
C'est le souffle du Juste,
qui rend plus bleu le ciel,
au-dessus des vallées.

Annaya

In countries of prayers
light inhabits a stained-glass window.
Morning in a chapel illuminates
a monk and his twin shadow.
The Virgin sleeps beneath her enamel.
The sun proclaims itself and toils
in the lands of St. Charbel.

In countries of prayers
a mountain has two profiles.
There are tears on the leaves of the poplars.
Between rocks you can harvest
flowers and beads for rosaries.

In countries of prayers
the moon abandons its orbit.
A child hides in the heather
four Our Fathers and one Hail Mary.

When night draws back her curtains,
a Carmelite passes
with a package of holy water and almonds from Jordan
in her bag.
The moon abandons its orbit
to brighten in a clearing
the brown robe of a hermit.

In countries of prayers
bodies are hostage to the same secret.
It is the breath of the Just
that beautifies the sky
above the valleys.

Balamand

Les Gens du Seigneur habitent un grand livre,
aux pages de pierre, aux lettres de cuivre.
Le nom est croisé, l'histoire byzantine,
le ciel par-dessus est bleu de glycine.
Les Gens du Seigneur lisent dans le vent,
tous les Ecrits Saints et le Testament.
Un Archimandrite mastique un Credo,
l'étoile qui brûle est un ex-voto.
Un œil de comète quelquefois embrase
le Pancréator dans l'Iconostase.
C'est à Balamand qu'on retrouve encore,
une odeur d'Antioche et de sycomore,
de foule impériale et du Chrysostome,
de Constantinople aux toits polychromes.
Un séminariste court sous le préau,
son ombre sautille comme un gros moineau.
Le couvent hiverne dans ses litanies,
et le Père Georges a des yeux d'hosties.
Les Gens du Seigneur parlent l'orthodoxe.
plantent des solstices et des équinoxes.
Et quand la montagne tout autour s'envole,
Les Gens du Seigneur servent de boussole.

Balamand

The people of the Lord inhabit a great book
with stone pages and letters of copper.
The name is Crusader, their story Byzantine,
and their sky wisteria-blue.
The people of the Lord read in the wind
the Holy Scriptures and the Testament.
An archemandrite mumbles a Credo,
and the ex-voto is a burning star.
Sometimes the eye of a comet sets
the Pancreator aflame in the Iconostase.
It is at Balamand that one can still find
the savor of Antioch, of sycamore,
of imperial crowds, of Chrysostom himself,
of Constantinople with its polychrome roofs.
A seminarian runs inside the cloisters,
his shadow sparrow-hopping behind him.
The monastery hibernates within its litanies,
and Father George has eyes like eucharistic hosts.
The people of the Lord speak Orthodox.
They plant solstices and equinoxes.
When the mountains around them wither,
the people of the Lord serve as a compass.

Baalbeck

Quand le soleil s'abat tel un grand arbre mort,
et que fleurit la lune,
les chemins de Baalbeck sentent le bleu des danses;
comme d'huile les choses enduites de silence.
La pierre et l'univers divulguent des secrets,
les souvenirs chevauchent comme lourds cavaliers;
traînent dans les sentiers prières et déités.
Et la nuit sort de ses cachots
comme un vautour d'un blanc repos,
Héliopolis et ses nuées.
Dessous chaque colonne, une étoile endormie
explose en deux novæ lorsque monte midi.
Le langage est lumière, le geste architecture,
Baalbeck est unité du monde des mesures.

Baalbeck

When the sun falls down like a tall dead tree
and when the moon blossoms,
the roads of Baalbeck know the blueness of dances;
things are coated with silence like oil.
Stones and the universe reveal secrets.
Memories ride on horseback like heavily armored knights,
pulling prayers and gods behind them down the roads.
Night comes out of its dark cell
like a vulture from a white repose—
Heliopolis under storm clouds.
Beneath each column a sleeping star
bursts into double novæ on the peak of noon.
Its language luminous, its gestures architectural,
Baalbeck is a gift from the world of measures.

Anjar

L'histoire lui a coupé la tête,
mais son corps de danseuse châtoie comme une fête,
en ce matin de la Békaa.
On dirait un vol de mouettes,
échoué dans quelque acacia:
ou peut-être un blanc paquebot,
sur un sommeil de coquelicot.
Anjar fut fille d'Omeyyades,
amie des caravanes et songe des nomades.
Du palais des Califes à la mosquée de Dieu,
l'araignée des chemins est dessin minutieux.
Anjar fut ville musulmane,
à l'enceinte sévère, à l'arcade rieuse;
hors ses murs une barbacane,
et dans ses patios une almée ingénieuse.
L'histoire lui a coupé la tête,
mais son corps de danseuse chatoie comme une fête,
en un matin de fantasia.

Il y eut ici des marchands,
venus de tous les coins du sang,
des vergers de l'Oronte et des plateaux afghans,
de terres situées hors de l'enclos du temps.

Il y eut ici des vents.
L'histoire lui a coupé la tête,
mais la lourde Békaa chatoie comme une fête,
en un matin d'Alleluia.

Anjar

History has cut off her head,
but her dancer's body gleams like a festival
at dawn in the Bekaa.
One might imagine that a flight of seagulls
had landed in acacias,
or is it a white steamship
in a slumber of poppies?
Anjar, the caravan's friend and the nomad's dream,
was the daughter of the Omeyyades.
From the palace of Caliphs to God's mosque,
its spiderweb of roads is a delicate, detailed design.
Anjar was a Moslem city
with sheer walls and a jubilant arcade;
beyond its walls, a barbican,
and on its patios, a brilliant almee dancing and singing.
History has cut off her head,
but her dancer's body gleams like a feast day
at the dawn of a dream.

Here there were merchants
gathered from all the corners of our blood,
from the orchards of Oronte, from Afghan plateaus,
from lands that lie beyond the will of time.

Here there were winds.
History has cut off her head,
but the generous Bekaa gleams like a feast
on the morning of glory.

Cèdres

Je vous salue,
vous qui êtes,
dans la simplicité d'une racine,
avec la nuit pour chien de garde.
Vos bruits ont la splendeur des mots,
et la fierté des cataclysmes.
Je vous connais,
vous qui êtes,
hospitaliers comme mémoire;
vous portez le deuil des vivants,
cars l'envers du temps, c'est le temps.
Je vous épèle,
vous qui êtes,
aussi uniques que le Cantique.
Un grand froid vous habille,
et le ciel à portée de branche.
Je vous défie,
vous qui hurlez sur la montagne
usant les syllabes jusqu'au sang.
Aujourd'hui c'est demain d'hier,
sur vos corps un astre couchant.
Je vous aime,
vous qui partez avec pour bannière le vent.
Je vous aime comme on respire,
vous êtes le premier Poème.

Cedars

I salute you,
you who draw life
from a single root
with the night as your watchdog.
Your rustlings have the splendor of words
and the supremacy of cataclysms.
I know you,
you who are
hospitable as memory;
you wear the grief of the living
because this side of time is time as well.
I spell your name,
you who are
unique as *The Song of Songs.*
A great cold enfolds you,
and heaven itself is in reach of your branches.
I defy you,
you who wail in our mountains
so that we hear the sounds in our blood.
Today, which is yesterday's tomorrow,
crosses your forms like a setting star.
I love you,
you who depart with the wind as your banner.
I love you as man loves breath.
You are the first poem.

Sud

Sud
ouvert comme une fenêtre par grand orage.
Sud
chaleureux comme un ancêtre,
inquiet comme un otage.
Sud
ma géographie à rebours,
cassable comme un grand amour,
que domine en conquistador,
l'ombre solaire de Beaufort.
Sud
au terrain docile, aux hommes turbulents,
qui, grands propriétaires, qui, noueux paysans,
intimes du tabac, bergers, et artisans,
précieux Rêveurs de Terre que le canon disloque,
et qui sont le début et la fin d'une époque.
Sud
à qui je voudrais promettre une Patrie,
et jardins opulents autour du Litani,
écrire des mots d'amour sur ton corps torturé,
offrir à tes enfants un soleil libanais.

South

South,
you are a window opened by a sudden storm.
South,
you are warm as an ancestor,
anxious as a hostage.
South,
you are my geography against change.
Fragile as a great love,
you dominate like a conquistador
the solar shades of Beaufort Castle.
South,
your gentle terrain holds turbulent men
who are great landowners, weathered farmers,
intimates of tobacco, shepherds and craftsmen,
precious earth-dreamers whom dogma banishes
but who are the alpha and omega of an era.
South,
I would like to promise you a homeland
and opulent gardens around the Litani,
to write with words of love on your tortured body,
to offer your children a Lebanese sun.

Promenade

Montagne ô bête magnifique,
nos racines dans ta crinière,
quatre saisons bien algébriques,
un cèdre bleu pour l'inventaire.
Lisse et royale la mer sans âge,
le vent doux comme un sacrement,
Dieu a troqué ses équipages
contre les cimes du Liban.

Montagnes ô Montagnes,
laissez-moi vous aimer
comme ceux qui n'ont pas d'âge sûr;
comme on égrène un chapelet
de légendes et de murmures.
Laissez-moi vous aimer,
à genoux comme le paysan et sa terre.
Doucement la lune sur le soir de vos chevelures.
Laissez-moi vous bercer
dans les muscles du vent chaud.
Alors la vaste paix,
mobile comme un scherzo.

IL FUT UN LIBAN DES JARDINS,
COMME IL EST UNE SAISON DOUCE.

Promenade

Mountain, you magnificent steed,
our roots grow in your mane
through four quite algebraic seasons
with one blue cedar as our inventory.
The ageless sea stands smooth and regal.
The wind is gentler than a sacrament.
For the summits of Lebanon
God must have bartered His retinue.

Mountains, my mountains,
let me love you
like those whose age is a mystery
or as one counts on beads
the retelling of legends and murmurs.
Let me love you
on my knees as a farmer loves his land.
Gently, with the moon on your thick hair's night,
let me rock you
in the sinews of the warm wind.
Then—a time of peace
lively as a scherzo.

ONCE THERE WAS A LEBANON OF THE GARDENS
JUST AS THERE IS A SEASON THAT IS TEMPERATE.

Sentimental Archives of a War in Lebanon

A Selection

❧

Archives sentimentales d'une guerre au Liban

Choix de poèmes

Translated by Paul B. Kelley

prologue

"Ils sont morts à plusieurs
C'est-à-dire chacun seul
sur une même potence qu'on nomme territoire
leurs yeux argiles ou cendres emportent la montagne
en otage de vie.

Alors la nuit
la nuit jusqu'au matin
puis de nouveau la mort
et leur souffle dernier dépose dans l'espace la fin du mot.

Quatre soleils montent la garde pour empêcher
le temps d'inventer une histoire.

Ils sont morts à plusieurs
sans se toucher
sans fleur à l'oreille
sans faire exprès
une voix tombe: c'est le bruit du jour sur le pavé.

Crois-tu que la terre s'habitue à tourner?
Pour plus de précision ils sont morts à plusieurs
par besoin de mourir
comme on ferme une porte lorsque le vent se lève
ou que la mer nous rentre par la bouche . . .

Alors
ils sont bien morts ensemble
c'est-à-dire chacun seul comme ils avaient vécu".

> *"Poèmes pour une histoire,"* 1972

Prologue

"They died as many
That is to say each one alone
on a gallows called territory
their clay or ashen eyes steal away the mountain
as hostage for life.

And then the night
night until the morning
then death once again
and their final breath utters forth the word's end.

Four suns stand guard lest
time invent a story.

They died as many
without two ever meeting
without a flower behind the ear
without intent
a voice falls away: the sound of day on the cobblestones.

Do you believe that the earth grows used to its rotation?
To be more precise they died as many
out of a need to die
like a door closed fast when the wind rises up
or when the sea gushes down our throats . . .

Then
they all died as one
that is to say each one alone just as they had lived."

"Poems for a Story," 1972

le jardin du consul

hier

"*Le droit d'aimer la terre est imprescriptible*"

"*Restez ne bougez pas*
pour raison de grandeur les ruines restent ruines . . ."

"*O que la vérité est menteuse*
car l'infini de l'eau est démenti par le sable.
Tout n'est si beau que parce que tout va mourir,
dans un instant."

"*Juin et les Mécréantes*"

The Consul's Garden

> *yesterday*

"The right to love the earth is inalienable"

"Stay; do not move
for reasons of grandeur the ruins remain ruins . . ."

"Oh how deceitful is truth
for the infinity of water is belied by the sand.
All things possess such beauty only because all will die,
in an instant."

> "June and the Miscreants"

J'habitais la maison d'en face,
face à la guerre et au Jardin,
de morts plantés et de rosiers,
ancêtres oubliés dans la dynamique d'une allée,
dans un cube de mémoire.
Sous le balcon d'un œil, une moitié de corps,
l'autre formant un angle sur le trottoir.
Une moitié de corps, signe isolé sur ma fresque de haine.

I lived in the house opposite
opposite the war and the Garden
of buried dead and rose bushes,
forgotten ancestors in the movement of a path,
in a cubic space of memory.
Beneath the balcony of an eye, half a body,
the other forming an angle on the pavement.
Half a body, lone sign upon my fresco of hate.

O Nuits élaborées
les Voyageurs d'Orient comptent vos politesses
sur les doigts d'une année.

Le vent et ses alliés
s'ouvrent tels une femme.
Et tout parle de tout.
Les bruits que j'imagine sont rivière ou sanglot.
O soleil de la nuit libre comme la mort,
on dirait cet instant où chacun se regarde.
Aussi ai-je enfermé sous ma langue un pays,
gardé comme une hostie.

Oh Nocturnal weavings,
the Voyagers of the Orient count your courtesies
upon the fingers of a year.

The wind and its allies
open themselves up just like a woman.
And all speaks of all.
The sounds I imagine are rivers or sobs.
Oh night sun as free as death,
as at that instant when each observes the other.
That is why I have stolen away underneath my tongue a land,
and kept it there like a host.

Cherchant la folie sous les sabots de nos rancunes,
nous avons prononcé les mots qui tuent.

J'avais l'âge de mes larmes,
et les voix de toutes mes mères.
Les maisons de mes amis avaient les joues rondes à Kantari.
La nuit je faisais des paquets d'étoiles filantes,
et je gagnais des guerres.
Quand la lumière rompait mon espace construit,
dessous les flamboyants,
tous les enfants,
tabliers bleus, souliers vernis,
et leurs noms dans la poche,
sortaient du ventre de leur chambre.
Derrière les légendes du jardin d'en face,
le Consul dans sa calligraphie violette,
faisait tinter des piastres religieuses.

Seeking madness beneath the clogs of our rancor,
we uttered the words that kill.

I possessed the age of my tears,
and the voices of all my mothers.
The homes of my friends had plump cheeks in Kantari.
At night I made parcels of shooting stars,
and won wars.
When the light splintered my sheltered space,
beneath the flame trees,
all the children,
in blue smocks and polished shoes,
and their names in their pockets,
were leaving the bowels of their rooms.
Behind the legends of the garden opposite,
the Consul with his purple calligraphy,
made religious piasters jingle.

La nuit, l'extrême nuit nous sillonne.
Arrogante comme un été.
Alors la durée nous mâche.

Soleil ô soleil,
éteint par l'eau du souvenir,
lorsque nous parcourions l'immobilité des jours,
à bord d'un regret.
De longitude en horizon,
le ciel une larme à la main.

Or tous les oiseaux exhalent un parfum de peur
et vont.

Un enfant démonte la voix lactée,
Aussitôt la paix du sang dans les jardins.
Gens aux yeux de sourcier
les arbres ont renié leurs branches,
comme hiver.

Dans la bouche noire des villes,
sonne le glas des fleurs.
Le pays est mort de beauté,
tué par un éclat de rire.
un obus dans la terre a creusé un sourire.

Night, darkest night runs through us.
Arrogant like the summer.
We are then devoured by time.

Sun, oh sun,
extinguished by the water of memory,
whilst we traveled through the stillness of the days,
alongside a regret.
From longitude to the horizon,
the sky a teardrop in the hand.

The birds exhale a scent of fear and take flight.

A child picks apart the Milky Way,
At once a blood peace throughout the gardens.
People with water diviner's eyes
the trees have disowned their branches,
like winter.

In the dark mouth of the cities,
tolls the death knell of the flowers,
The land has died of beauty,
killed by a burst of laughter.
A bombshell in the ground has hollowed out a smile.

Nous nous sommes battus
pour le plaisir d'apprendre
l'orgueil de mourir.

Débris de vent,
calme chétif des matins
entre deux morceaux de ville.
"Combats acharnés".
"Nouvelles médiations".
"Parties concernées".
Lynche nos vingt ans l'asphalte des routes,
qui vont de l'espoir jusqu'à la violence,
tout comme autrefois,
nos adolescences.
L'autre camp (peut-on choisir sa démence?)
saigne de mille roses.
ON TIRE SUR UNE IDÉE ET L'ON ABAT UN HOMME
Toujours écarlate la puissance des mots,
plus meurtriers qu'un geste.
Ceux qui vivent au soleil de la parole,
au cheval emballé des slogans,
ceux-là,
brisent les vitres de l'univers.

We fought one another
for the pleasure of learning
the arrogance of dying.

Debris of wind,
feeble calm of the morning
between two parts of town.
"Fierce combat."
"New mediations."
"Factions concerned."
The asphalt of the roads leading from hope to violence
lynches our twenty years,
just as erstwhile,
our adolescence.
The opposing side (can one choose one's madness?)
bleeds a thousand roses.
AN IDEA IS SHOT AND A MAN DROPS DEAD.
Always scarlet red the power of words,
more murderous than a gesture.
Those who live in the sunlight of the word,
upon the runaway horse of slogans,
those,
shatter the windows of the universe.

Comme il est triste que souvent
l'image coupe la parole.
Silex contre silex
deux pensées et leur angle.

Ceux qui sont morts ont droit,
à un grand portrait noir
sur un beau mur tout blanc,
au souvenir du jour de l'an,
au discours de vivants.
La douce amie d'hier,
talons aiguille et jupe au vent,
mêle une larme, à la sueur
de ses nouveaux amants.
Ceux qui sont morts n'ont pas une odeur de printemps.

De grand oiseaux brossaient le ciel
au petit jour; et du corps des amants,
lentement, la rosée comme une prière.
A Beyrouth, la guerre.

How sad it is that often times
the image cuts short the word.
Flint against flint
two thoughts and their angle.

Those who have died are entitled
to a great black portrait
upon a blank wall,
to a New Year's remembrance,
to the words of the living.
The gentle friend of yesterday,
stiletto heels and skirt blowing in the wind,
mingles a teardrop, with the sweat
of her new lovers.
Those who are dead have no scent of springtime.

Great birds rose up against the sky
at daybreak; and from lovers' bodies,
slowly, morning dew like a prayer.
War in Beirut.

folle terre

ensuite

Foolish Land

later

Ecoute,
toi dont la voix fait de grands gestes,
et dont les bras sont chant d'oiseau,
écoute: la ville blanche est un tombeau.
Ne crains ni le soir ni l'ennui,
tous deux ouvrent sur un jardin.
Ne crains ni l'amour ni la nuit,
la mort est un chariot faisant route vers l'est,
la vie n'est que la vie, simple abri du regard.
Ecoute.
Il y a sur ton ombre des chemins de quiétude.
Absolue.

Listen,
you whose voice makes great gestures
and whose arms are birdsong,
listen: the white city is a tomb.
Fear neither evening nor ennui,
both open on to a garden.
Fear neither love nor night,
death is a chariot heading east,
life is but life, a mere refuge for the eyes.
Listen.
There lie upon your shadow paths of tranquility.
Absolute.

En plein soleil,
avec le vent autour du cou
et fouets de pluie dans la bouche,
en plein soleil,
je regarde suinter les murs de ma mémoire.
Tu es celui qui, à trois pas,
m'as tendu ses cheveux pour que je m'y accroche.
Fais-donc voler toutes ces balles
qui tuent ou ne tuent pas selon des règles de tendresse.
Lâche-moi à présent,
car je chavire de l'autre côté de mon ventre
rouge du sang de tous.
Et je ris en plein soleil,
parce que la folie moissonne le paysage,
studieusement.
Même toi à trois pas mets un hiver sur ton visage
pour m'arracher mon souffle et
l'accrocher à la frontière d'à côté.
Alors en plein soleil
je meurs d'incohérence
en éclats.

In the heat of the sun,
with the wind round my neck
and rain whipping at my mouth,
in the heat of the sun,
I watch the walls of my memory sweat.
It was you who, just a step away,
held out your hair so that I might cling to it.
Discard, then, all these bullets
that kill or do not kill according to the rules of tenderness.
Now, let go of me,
for I am sent reeling, my womb
red with the blood of us all.
And I laugh in the heat of the sun,
because madness garners the landscape,
studiously.
Even you just a step away wear winter upon your face
so as to wrest from me my life's breath
and hang it over the border.
So in the heat of the sun
I die of incoherence
in bursts.

Je sais la géométrie d'un parfum,
la couleur aimée d'une odeur (rouge)
La mort a le même poids que la peur,
et ma poitrine mille mémoires.
Des frontières bougent sous ma peau
qui regarde la nuit
d'un oeil vif de langouste (180°).
Or
la forte terre me garde dans ses organes,
mais,
l'oiseau boite sur le ciel.
Et je sais pour conclure,
l'espace étriqué d'un amour.

I know the geometry of a scent,
the loved color of a (red) odor
Death has the same weight as fear,
and my breast a thousand memories.
Borders shift under my skin
watching the night
with the crawfish's quick eye (180°).
Now
the mighty earth holds me in her organs,
but,
the bird limps along in the sky.
And I know, to conclude,
the narrow space of a romance.

Je suis ou ne suis pas, selon la loi du rêve,
mais forcément siège du Temps.
Mon coeur a de partout vue sur ville et charnier,
lorsque l'Orient nocturne,
dans sa douce puissance,
retrouve par les mots le chemin du silence,
dont le nom guerrier est fracas.
J'inonderai de vie le soleil et sa course,
car ma Terre est de porcelaine.
Je suis ou ne suis pas, selon un vieux remords,
vos corps ont forme de deux mondes
sur la nuque de la Grande Ourse.
Pays donc,
je t'offre la mort.

I am or am not, depending on the law of dreams,
but of necessity the seat of Time.
My heart has looked down upon town and charnel-house,
while Orient of night,
with its sweet power,
finds once again through words the path of silence,
whose warrior name is a deafening roar.
I shall inundate with life the sun and its orbit,
for my Earth is porcelain.
I am or am not, depending on an ancient remorse,
your bodies take the shape of two worlds,
resting upon the nape of Ursa Major.
So my country,
I bestow upon you death.

Je tisserai lumière dans ces montagnes;
et la nommerai liberté—
nom commun à trop de visages—
J'entendrai galoper vos doutes,
flanc contre flanc de minaret,
contre entrailles d'église;
et je saurai que désormais
jamais plus, VRAI, ne sera, JUSTE;
et je rirai de voir pousser
l'herbe violente de la guerre.
O cette haine,
ô cette haine qui féconde la terre,
comme sang chaud de femme.
O cet amour,
ô cet amour sous mes canines,
comme grain rond de cardamone.
O tendresse-brouillard,
sur le Liban comme cortège.
Pays vieux,
souvenir nécessaire de ces corps mutilés
qui te font légitime.
L'histoire est debout sur ta plage,
quand bat le pouls de ma montagne.

I shall weave light in these mountains,
and name it liberty—
a name shared by too many faces—
I will hear your doubts galloping,
flank pressed against minaret flank,
against church bowels;
and will know that henceforth
never again will TRUE be JUST;
and I will laugh to see grow
the violent grass of war.
Oh this hate,
oh this hate that fecundates the earth,
like a woman's warm blood.
Oh this love,
oh this love under my canines,
like a round grain of cardamom.
Oh tenderness-fog,
hanging upon Lebanon like a funeral cortège.
Ancient land,
vital memory of these mutilated bodies
that legitimize you.
History stands erect upon your shores,
while my mountain's pulse beats.

le futur de mon temps

anjourd'hui

The Future of My Time

today

J'ai le coeur dans les tempes et le front à hauteur des cimes de ma tribu.
L'évidence du souvenir prend forme de cordon ombilical, arrimé à chaque
visage, et des larmes de retrouvailles montent hautes, derrière le barrage de
mes yeux. Tout cela s'explique par l'entente de l'homme avec le paysage. Ils
font partie du même poème.

Alors tandis que le soir trace dans la nuit du ciel des mots de bienvenue, les
vents du Mont-Liban m'enveloppent d'une douce colère.

J'appartiens à ma folle terre : je la crée par ma mort, et son visage brûle de
mille regards plus incandescents que la faim.

Je ne suis libre que de sa permanence.

Intacte de toute parole étrangère à ses lois.

Je demeure, dans la volupté du prisonnier, parcourue par ses mains
retrouvées, prêtresses de toutes mes vies.

Je survis à ma propre poussière, et connais de mémoire le futur de mon
temps.

My heart throbs in my temples as my gaze looks over the summits of my tribe. Memories take the form of an umbilical cord, attached to every face, and tears of painful reunions well up, behind the barrier of my eyes. All this is explained by man's harmony with the landscape. They are part of the same poem.

So while evening traces words of welcome in the night sky, the winds of Mount Lebanon shroud me in a sweet anger.

I belong to my foolish land: I create it through my death, and its face is consumed by a thousand gazes more incandescent than hunger.

Its permanence alone makes me free.

Intact from all words foreign to its laws.

I remain, in a prisoner's exquisite delight, traveled through length and breadth by its regained hands, priestesses of my every life.

I survive my own ashes, and know from memory the future of my time.

Je baisse la voix pour mieux entendre
hurler Pays; pour dire le mal
de n'avoir planté ni amour ni haine,
d'avoir mélangé les racines,
et pris pour montagne la mer.
Je baisse la voix pour aiguiser
les couteaux du tonnerre,
demander force à la tribu,
dormir entre ses omoplates de rochers.
J'habite le silence
pour mieux contrôler le pouls de la race,
dire que, s'il faut mourir,
c'est à cause d'une seule goutte de sang,
différente.

I lower my voice to better hear
the Country howl; to utter the sorrow
of having planted neither the seed of love nor hate,
of having mixed the roots,
and confused the mountain with the sea.
I lower my voice to sharpen
the knives of thunder,
to ask for strength from the tribe,
to sleep between its rocky shoulder blades.
I inhabit the silence
to better regulate the race's pulse,
to say that, if I must die,
it is on account of a single drop of blood,
not mine.

Je ne crains qu'une loi
celle de la mise au ban.
Refusant tout autre stigmate,
Je suis berger de mes vices,
allumeur de bûchers, sur le corps de l'Histoire.
Je baisse la voix pour mieux entendre
les multiples de mon appartenance,
et les choyer, ô les comprendre,
et savoir, que multiple veut dire, Pays,
Semblables et non semblables,
ô fleurs d'un même ciel,
oiseaux d'un même climat,
et vaisseaux d'un même âge,
nous,
au bord du Moyen-Orient.

.

I fear but one law
that of banishment.
Refusing all other stigmata,
I am shepherd of my vices,
lighter of funeral pyres, upon the body of History.
I lower my voice to better hear
the multiples of my belonging,
to pamper them, understand them,
and know that multiple means Country.
Similar and dissimilar,
oh flowers of a self-same sky,
birds of a single climate,
and vessels of one age,
together as one,
upon the shores of the Middle East.

Suis-je né d'un mensonge
dans un pays qui n'existait pas?

Suis-je tribu au confluent de sangs contraires?

Mais peut-être ne suis-je pas.
Certes je ne suis pas, vos équations le disent,
même en baissant la voix je n'entends pas la mer,
ni n'entends la lumière.
Qui me rendra présent?
Menacé, donc vivant,
blessé, donc étant
peureux, donc effrayant,
debout, donc flamboyant.

Qui me rendra présent?

Was I born of a lie
in a country that did not exist?

Am I one tribe at the confluence of two opposing bloods?

But perhaps I am not.
But of course I am not, your equations prove it,
even while lowering my voice I do not hear the sea,
nor do I hear the light.
Who will make me real?
Threatened, therefore living,
Wounded, therefore being,
Fearful, therefore frightening,
Erect, therefore a flame tree.

Who will make me real?

Je ne suis peut-être que passant strident,
cherchant racine du nom de Terre,
promeneur du vide,
explorateur de regrets,
mais,
je baisse la voix pour mieux entendre
hurler-Pays,
entendre les chiens de la mort
ivres de la première blessure,
qui seule fut pure, car libre.

O bruit du délire qui prend forme de mer,
pensées ourlant l'émeute des heures.

Nous naissons menacés de vie,
et le demeurons,
jusqu'à ce que conjointement,
menace et vie nous quittent.

I am perhaps but a shrill passer-by,
seeking roots by the name of Earth,
stroller of the void,
explorer of regrets,
but,
I lower my voice to hear more clearly
the Country-howl,
to hear the dogs of death
drunk from the initial wound,
that, because it was free, was alone pure.

O sound of delirium that takes the shape of the sea,
thoughts hemming the riot of the hours.

We are born threatened with life,
and remain so,
until from us jointly,
threat and life depart.

après-propos

Qui dira le gué traversé par mes yeux?
L'effroi du regard évitant son semblable?
Si la mort n'est pas contemporaine de folie,
qui dira l'horreur consanguine,
de n'être plus que des hordes,
à la jonction des vents?

afterword

Who shall tell of the ford that my eyes have waded through?
The terror of the gaze avoiding its fellow creature?
If death is not contemporaneous with madness,
who shall tell of the horror of blood relations,
reduced to nothing more than hordes,
where the winds meet?

pour g.t.

En ce temps
rien n'était frugal :
ni Mort, ni Vie.
La parole mettait dans nos veines,
le carillon de la démence.
Ciel épais d'Orient,
éteins ta lampe et cette étoile,
pour donner pleine-nuit au meurtre.
Et si moi je ne peux que le matin absolve
ces assassins aux noms d'enfants.
En ce temps
rien n'était frugal.
A quelques jambes du prisonnier
veille un sanglot.

Avons-nous dans nos coeurs d'asphalte
vécu le feu et sa débauche ?
Avons-nous posté sentinelles
au péristyle de nos rêves
et pendu nos oiseaux à tous les méridiens ?

Avons-nous enchaîné le vent ?

Au temps où
rien n'était frugal
nous avons sabordé la Terre.

17 février 1982

for g.t.

At that time
Nothing was sparing:
Neither Death, nor Life.
The spoken word put in our veins,
the carillon of madness.
Thick sky of Orient,
extinguish your lamp and this star,
to give the darkness of night to murder.
And if I cannot, may the morning absolve
these murderers with children's names.
At that time
nothing was sparing.
A few feet from the prisoner
a sob keeps vigil.

Have we in our asphalt hearts
lived through the fire and its orgy?
Have we posted sentinels
at the peristyle of our dreams
and hanged our birds from every meridian?

Have we enslaved the wind?

At the time when
nothing was sparing
we scuttled the Earth.

            17 February 1982

Home, Politics, and Exile

SYRINE C. HOUT

❧In her essay "Modernist Poetry in Arabic," Salma Jayyusi demon-strates why and how Arabic poetry, in the span of about five decades in the twentieth century, passed through stages almost identical to those that Western poetry had undergone over the last three centuries (138). Most notable among myriad stylistic and thematic innovations "all over the Arab world from Bahrain to Morocco" (179) was the transformation of vision and tone around 1980. Despite the national disasters constituted by the creation of Israel in 1948 and the Six Day War of June 1967, the hope for Pan-Arab solidarity prompted most pre-1980s poets in their writings to champion resistance against Zionism while promoting domes-tic political change. But the faith in individual and collective revolutionary action eventually gave way to "silence or exile, and an atmosphere of frustration and passive anger" (178). The poets of the 1980s severed all bonds with traditional values, invariably re-flecting both skepticism and pessimism about the present and the future.

The Lebanese civil war (1975–1989) contributed in no small part to this sense of defeat. Lebanese poetry, whether written in Arabic or in French, dealt with the irrationality and tragic reality of internal strife. In the Francophone tradition, most war-inspired po-etry was supplied by women writers (Jabbour 1997, 16–17). This phenomenon is not surprising because the heyday of women's po-etry began in the '60s (Anhoury 113). The complementary but often contradictory sentiments of exile and national belonging, characteristic of modern poetry in general (84), became at once much more prominent and far more nuanced after 1975, the watershed year that ushered in the fourth developmental phase of Francophone Lebanese literature (Jabbour 1997, 7).[1]

Spanning twenty years (1963–83), Nadia Tuéni's publications illustrate two phases of experience, her first five pre-1975 collections and her last two poetic works, *Liban:Vingt poèmes pour un amour* (1979) and *Archives sentimentales d'une guerre au Liban* (1982) (Jabbour 1992, 15–16).[2] Unlike her earlier poems, the later ones exhibit not so much a spiritual quest as a search for personal identity inevitably entangled with that of Lebanon, a nation caught in a vicious circle of religious hatred and senseless violence. Here, the nation is more than a reservoir of images; it has evolved into a geographical reality as well as a socio-historical space in Tuéni's engaged poetry (124). Miriam Cooke states that Tuéni's major concern is the effect that the war has had "on the individual's relationship to, and identity with, the land" (164). Exile, used often as an antonym for "homeland" and generally manifesting itself in physical and/or psychological terms, is experienced when the connection to one's native soil is put to the test in extreme and abnormal situations, such as war.

Several critics have read Tuéni's writings as a poetic quest strongly influenced by personal life experiences, most notably the demise of her seven-year-old daughter Nayla in 1963 and her own battle against cancer. Focusing on philosophical, psychological, and symbolic elements, Jad Hatem calls her oeuvre an interior voyage toward a new God and a new Promised Land (23). Zahida Jabbour sees in Tuéni a poet destined to permanent wandering and searching for a niche at a time when her nation was a reality only in exile

1. Periodization is determined by the identity of political power in Lebanon. The first three stages are 1874–1920 (Ottoman rule), 1920–1943 (French mandate), and 1943–1975 (national independence).

2. Several of Tuéni's poems have been translated into Arabic, English, and Spanish. Her last two works were recorded on cassettes, produced by "Le Domaine Musical de Chambray" (Ed. Valois) in Paris in 1984. The recital of *Archives sentimentales d'une guerre au Liban* is accompanied by music.

(1992, 37). Referring to her posthumous collection *La Terre arrêtée,* the same critic comments, "Manhattan, New York, Petra and Jarash, Cairo and Beirut are vividly presented" (178).[3] Overall, her corpus is grounded in "the Lebanese mountains, in the sand and the desert, in Jericho and the Negev, in Greece and the Mediterrannean" (210). Born to a Lebanese Druze father and a French Christian mother and having spent several adolescent years in Greece, Tuéni saw herself at the confluence of multiple cultures—equally exposed to the Orient and the Occident, open to both the desert and the sea (1987, 103). Lebanon's largest asset, in her judgment, is its cultural pluralism, making it "the opposite of a ghetto." Furthermore, she asserts, the ability to enjoy various influences is the ability to live with the manifold (104).

What happens, however, if and when cultural and religious pluralism[4] no longer yields diversity but metamorphoses instead into a breeding ground for factionalism and fanaticism? In this essay I concentrate on the exilic nature of, and exilic sentiment in, *Archives sentimentales d'une guerre au Liban.*[5] Of special concern will be the semantic ambiguities of home and homeland and the changing boundaries of the "here" and "there," as illustrated in images of attachment to, and withdrawal from, Lebanese soil. In an attempt to determine these boundaries, I trace the meanings of several recurrent keywords indicative of space, namely, Lebanon, Beirut, Kantari, Mount Lebanon, the Middle East, the Orient, landscape, country, and earth. Throughout this essay, my reading will juxtapose the personal and the political.

After the outbreak of the Lebanese war, Nadia accompanied her husband Ghassan Tuéni first to Paris and later to Washington,

3. I have provided my own translations of all citations from French-language studies as well as from Tuéni's poetry.

4. Lebanon has seventeen official religious denominations.

5. All page citations of *Archives sentimentales d'une guerre au Liban* refer to Tuéni's *Les Oeuvres poétiques complètes,* ed. Jad Hatem (Beirut: Dar An-Nahar, 1986).

D.C., and New York, where he served as Lebanon's ambassador to the United Nations from 1977 to 1982, the year in which she returned to Lebanon significantly weakened by cancer. In North America, Tuéni's horizons were enlarged. At that point, the "whole earth served as her promenade gallery. Greece, Paris, Washington, and New York: all became her property, her nation" (Fakhouri 1998, 126). Tuéni was on some level a citizen of the world without ever relinquishing her primal love for Lebanon, the country in which she was born and raised, married, spent many years of her adult life, and died at the age of forty-eight. The end came after she had despaired of this "savage exile" (Fakhouri 187). For Tuéni, exile and homeland clearly went beyond conventional definitions to encompass shifting psychological realities, often reflective of larger but equally unstable political ones.

Archives sentimentales d'une guerre au Liban was written in New York and published in Paris by Editions Pauvert in 1982, the seventh year of the war and one that witnessed the Israeli invasion on June 6, exactly fifteen years after the debacle of June 1967. Tuéni died on June 20, 1983, after a fifteen-year struggle with cancer. The correspondence of dates and periods is coincidental, but it is suggestive of the intimate link between the private and the political in her poetry. In the same year, she wrote of the fate she shared with her "foolish" country in expiating "a crime of double identity" *(Prose,* 253).

As the last work to be published during Tuéni's lifetime, *Archives sentimentales d'une guerre au Liban* has been read as a "product of disappointment" (Fakhouri 1998, 36) and an "awakening to the truth," dramatizing a "philosophy, a doctrine, and an attitude toward the war" (Jabbour 1992, 143–44). In attempting to understand the catastrophic and anarchic present, the poems serve as "an exorcism" in the hope (against hope) of symbolically recapturing a sense of peace and harmony (Sami Anhoury, quoted in Anhoury 1987, 146). Hatem reads the work as a transsubstantiation of the country (94). The epigrams preceding the prologue and the three subsequent chapters are borrowed from *Juin et les mécréantes* (1968) and therefore express "disillusion, foreseeing a future death, the end of an age" (Jabbour 1992, 144). Arguably, they also reveal an attempt at connecting, in structural and poetic terms, the reflections of, as well as the meditations on, the past and present that would otherwise seem more random and fragmentary. Like the intermittent although unpredictable nature of political unrest in the Middle East—a fact suggested by the recurring citations from the earlier work with the prologue excerpted from *Poèmes pour une histoire* (1972)—the links between the past, the present, and the future in *Archives sentimentales d'une guerre au Liban* are constructed with the help of personal but also collective memory and imagination.

The title combines the personal and the collective in the phrase "sentimental archives." The word "archives" is defined as either "a place where documents and other materials of public or historical importance are preserved" or the documents themselves *(Random House* 1991, 72). Therefore, the work itself may be viewed either as the home for these (re)collections or as a body of verse in the larger tradition of antiwar literature. The adjective "sentimental" is polyvalent because it encompasses attitude, opinion, thought, and emotion, often that of nostalgia (1222). The indefinite article used for war (in Lebanon) hints at its chronicity and, paradoxically, its indistinctness.

In the opening line of the first poem in part 1, "Le jardin du consul" ("The Consul's Garden") subtitled "hier" ("Yesterday"), the poet recreates the scene of the house she inhabited facing the consul's garden in Beirut's opulent Kantari neighborhood. Jabbour sees the consul as representing the tranquil and prosperous period between 1840 and 1860 in Lebanese history, a lost paradise and a mythical universe of symbiosis between subject and object, where memory and imagination are almost one (1992, 155–57). Tempting as it may be to isolate and hence to protect this vision in the poet's "cube de mémoire" ("cube of memory," Tuéni 1986, 301) from ensuing chaos, I disagree with this overly contrastive reading on three counts: the political significance of the consul, the position of the poet-as-subject, and the consul's garden/house as object of her gaze. Two bits of extratextual evidence, one of which is provided by the same critic, support my interpretation. Tuéni's scenes and characters in "The Consul's Garden," which she initially intended to use as raw material for a novel, are at least partly grounded in reality (Jabbour 1992, 162). Furthermore, in a letter addressed to a student and dated June 1979, Tuéni described her then-evolving work *Archives sentimentales d'une guerre au Liban* as consisting of poems whose décor is that of 1936, when Lebanon was still under a French mandate that ended in 1943, and 1976, by which time the war that led to her exile was well underway *(Prose, 1986, 104).*

A consul, by definition, is "an official appointed by the government of a country to look after its commercial interests and the welfare of its citizens in another country" *(Random House* 1991, 292). In this capacity, he represents foreign diplomatic power and influence on Lebanese soil in times of international peace and cultural interchange. The poet observes the transactions in the "garden" and on the "sidewalk" from her "balcony" *(Oeuvres poetiques complètes,* 301). These locations are semi-open spaces: gardens and balconies are external appendages to homes in the same manner that sidewalks separate streets from rows of buildings. The garden is "espace réservé à l'histoire" ("space reserved for history," *Poetry* 1986, 302) because the spring ball it hosts at night is both a private and a public event, an archive of sentimental but also of political stability in the early chapters of the poet's and Lebanon's existence. The garden, mentioned five times in part 1, is in the heart of Kantari, which is mentioned three times and is a central vicinity in the capital Beirut, which itself appears once in the last line of the chapter. "[L]a guerre" ("[T]he war"), the final phrase following "Beyrouth," has now disrupted this concentric arrangement of radial harmony.

In the middle of the Muslim holy month of Ramadan—a time of piety and forgiveness—the consul, a lover of arabesque "sur la géographie du Liban" ("on the geography of Lebanon," 305), registers his complaint on a piece of paper about those who "aiment le bruit du bruit" ("love the noise of noise," 304). Like the nomad at night and the migrating bird, he too must leave. Similarly, the poet's young friends and schoolchildren in their blue uniforms and shiny shoes are ejected "du ventre de leur chambre" ("from the belly of their room," 306), and the birds "exhalent un parfum de peur et vont" ("exhale a perfume of fear and go," 307). This age—marking the loss of innocence, forced departures, and the rupture of the poet's "espace construit" ("constructed space," 306)—witnesses the division of the city into "deux morceaux" ("two pieces," 308).

The appearance of the vice-consul (in the ninth poem) as a delegate, or a substitute, signals a bureaucratic and perhaps an ideological transition; his speech on the verandah about the dangers of factional language is akin to a sermon from the pulpit: the space he indicates widens here to encompass the "terre d'orient" ("land of the Orient") and that of the "Moyen-Orient" ("Middle East," 309). Whereas the "Orient" is the product as well as the organizing principle of what Edward Said refers to as "imaginative geography"— that which helps the Western mind "intensify its own sense of itself by dramatizing the distance and difference between what is close to it and what is far away" (1979, 55)—"Middle East" is a more recent term and a political one. Although I do not mean to suggest that the vice-consul, or the consul for that matter, is an orientalist in the pejorative sense of the term, the former does appear as Egeria, the Roman goddess of fountains and of childbirth (i.e., of life), wearing gloves while changing the contours of the Middle East. Gloves are worn for reasons of fashion, self-protection, and sometimes self-concealment. In an ironic gesture presenting these figures as skilled orators speechifying about the power of speech in Lebanon to others, Tuéni may be alluding here to the invisible hands that have shaped the political map of the region. The paradoxical phrase "la haine de son amitié" ("the hatred of his friendship," 309) preceding this poem reveals at best the ambivalent, and at worst the duplicitous, nature of foreign policy. Corroborating my interpretation is

Mona Amyuni's reading of the consul's ball as a satire of consulates which represent major powers by playing around with smaller countries as peons on a checkerboard (145 46).

Part 2, "folle terre" ("foolish land"), is subtitled "ensuite" ("later"), a temporally noncommittal word referring to neither yesterday (the past) nor today (the present) but to sometime in-between. The focus is no longer on an urban garden circumscribed in time and space; it has widened to encompass a chunk of earth tinged with madness and noise. In the first poem (312) the poet tries to restore her sense of balance by seeking refuge in the harmony of nature: "le rythme de la vague" ("the rhythm of the wave"), "la couleur des grands fonds" ("the color of the great deeps"), "la mathématique exacte des mouettes" ("the exact mathematics of seagulls"), and "le talent des planètes" ("the talent of planets"). But nature falls short of providing open vistas now that "nous avons fabriqué un ciel sphérique" ("we have fabricated a spherical sky," 312). The white city is sepulchral, its garden anonymous, and death is "un chariot faisant route vers l'est" ("a chariot making its way east," 313). It is as if life itself has been chased away or snuffed out from the city, no longer mentioned by name. Death, however, is not confined to the city, for "la folie moissonne le paysage, studieusement" ("madness is gathering in the landscape, studiously," 314), leaving the poet reddened by everyone's blood. The garden/granary from which memories are derived are no longer terrestrial but synonymous with the star. But hope for continued life on earth ebbs with the onslaught of sunlight. The poet senses "des frontières" ("frontiers," 316) moving under her skin. While the strong earth keeps her inside its organs, the bird, the symbol of freedom, limps through the sky in the same manner the poet feels trapped in the "espace étriqué" ("cramped space," 316) of love.

The seventh poem (317) contains several peregrine images of the poet's desire to break out of her narrow range of mobility: "je navigue en sommeil, / vers les mêmes peurs familières / de cheraux sauvages" ("I navigate in sleep / toward the familiar fears / of wild horses"). She wishes to "errer" ("roam") in the eyes of her addressee, where the earth drowns and she could bloom once again in a marine orchard. The addressee's lips are the equator and a kingdom in Africa, while the teeth are the tombstones. This being, the poet's Other, offers the supplicant the possibility, or at least the illusion, of an alternative existence, an exilic life akin to death. The eighth poem (318) takes us back to the city, equivalent to a mass grave. The nocturnal Orient "dans sa douce puissance, retrouve par les mots le chemin du silence, dont le nom guerrier est fracas" ("in its sweet power, finds again with words the road of silence, whose war name is din"). Here, the poet may be hinting at the silent indifference of Arab countries, contrasted with the racket caused by falling bodies on Lebanon's "Terre de porcelaine" ("Earth . . . of porcelain").

Addressing the night toward the end of the tenth poem, the poet exclaims, "j'habiterai ma mémoire" ("I will live in my memory," 319), echoing the first line in *Archives sentimentales d'une guerre au Liban*: "J'habitais la maison d'en face" ("I lived in the opposite house," 301). This introverted move equates the house of childhood with the memory of that abode. Refuge in a tangible location is no longer possible. Even the mountains hesitate between the earth and the sea. The erosion of harmony from the natural and social worlds turns the poet into a spiritual vagabond whose eyes "iront au galop chercher un lieu de démesure" ("will go at a gallop looking for a place of excess," 319). Gardens have become a "[t]hème, sur les plages de nos mémoires" ("theme, on the beaches of our memories," 320). In the twelfth poem, Lebanon is a "[p]ays vieux" ("[o]ld country," 321) whose soil, fertilized by confessional hatred, yields the violent grass of war. The ashes, which the poet loves, taste of a city that supersedes the ancient Oriental and imperial cities of Antioch and Babylon.[6] Heated speech and folly have burned all. In the

6. Amyuni interprets "archives" as referring to the multiple historical, linguistic, cultural, and sentimental strata of the city of Beirut (199).

last poem peace, freedom, and love are relegated to a world beyond and above "le croissant rouge des batailles" ("the red crescent of battles," 324) embodied by the dead yet free female infant[7] on the other side of the wall.

"Le futur de mon temps"("the future of my time") is transformed into the present by the subtitle "aujourd'hui" ("today") in part 3. Future and present are one, as are the poet and her "folle terre" ("foolish land," 326), two equations declaring the end of hope. Today, she "habite le silence" ("lives in silence," 327), after having dwelled in her childhood home (part 1) and in her memory (part 2). This development signifies her increasing alienation from her roaring, seismic country. Nonetheless, she does not fall into apathy. The third poem (329) delivers an oblique critique of the political indifference of Arab countries toward the Lebanese tragedy. She asks "les pleureuses" ("the weepers") to dry their "larmes de pétrole, filles des larmes d'or, et alliées aux larmes de fer" ("tears of oil, daughters of the tears of gold, allies of the tears of iron"). The concern displayed by rich oil countries is insincere and motivated by selfish interests, not by sympathy or the sense of a common destiny. But the dying country is not ready for interment, and the empty sarcophagus shows lingering hope, at least for today. In the fourth poem (329), the poet declares her only fear to be that of the law sanctioning "la mise au ban" ("banishment"). In this "multiple Pays" ("multiple . . . Country") "au bord du Moyen-Orient" ("on the edge of the Middle East"), the fear of expulsion and subsequent isolation is shared by all citizens.

The sixth poem is permeated with doubt about identity and belonging. Even the country's existence is questioned. The seventh poem attempts an answer, albeit a sad one. For succor, the poet turns to the "fictive montagne, installée dans les limbes de la géographie" ("fictitious mountain, installed in the limbo of geography,"

---

7. Critics have seen this figure as representing Tuéni's deceased daughter.

332). She demands that it revivify her and grant her love and recognition. The mountain holds some promise for personal,[8] but more importantly, for symbolic reasons. Unlike man-made cities, mountains are natural and thus enduring. In "[t]erre de trop de gens et Terre de personne" ("[l]and of too many people and Land of nobody," 332), the poet has lost her anchor: she is a "passant strident, cherchant racine du nom de Terre, promeneur du vide, explorateur de regrets") ("strident passer-by, looking for roots of the name Earth, stroller of the void, explorer of regrets," 333).

The last poem in *Archives sentimentales d'une guerre au Liban* ends on a seemingly pessimistic note: the threatening nature of life itself, increased by the added menace imposed by war, can only be overcome by the extinction of life. Paradoxically, death becomes both exit and entrance: permanent exile from life, i.e., death, provides spiritual serenity in an eternal abode. The "après-propos" ("afterword")[9] equates life and death with excess. Although the poet is unable to either forgive or forget the sins of the "assassins" (335), she hopes that the new morning, possibly the next generation, will do so after a long night of barbarity.

Works Cited

Amyuni, Mona Takieddine. 1998. *La Ville source d'inspiration: Le Caire, Khartoum, Beyrouth, Paola Scala chez quelques écrivains arabes contemporains. Beiruter Texte und Studien.* Vol. 63. Gen. Ed. Angelika Neuwirth. Beirut: Orient-Institut.

Anhoury, Najwa Aoun. 1987. *Panorama de la poésie libanaise d'expression française.* Beirut: Dar El-Machreq.

Cooke, Miriam. 1987. *War's Other Voices: Women Writers on the Lebanese Civil War.* Cambridge: Cambridge Univ. Press.

8. Tuéni was born in Baakline, a town in Lebanon's Shuf mountains.
9. It is addressed to Ghassan Tuéni and dated February 17, 1982.

Fakhouri, Nelly H. 1998. *La Quaternité de la parole poétique de Nadia Tuéni*. Beirut: Dar An-Nahar.

Hatem, Jad. 1987. *La Quête poétique de Nadia Tuéni*. Beirut: Dar An-Nahar.

Jabbour, Zahida Darwiche. 1997. *Etudes sur la poésie libanaise francophone: Abi Zeyd, Naffah, Schéhadé, Stétié, Hatem*. Beirut: Dar An-Nahar.

————. 1992. *Poésie et initiation dans l'oeuvre de Nadia Tuéni*. Beirut: Dar An-Nahar.

Jayyusi, Salma Khadra. 1992. "Modernist Poetry in Arabic." *Modern Arabic Literature*. Ed. M. M. Badawi. Cambridge: Cambridge Univ. Press, 132–79.

Random House Webster's College Dictionary. 1991. McGraw-Hill Edition. New York: Random House.

Said, Edward W. 1979. *Orientalism*. New York: Vintage.

Tuéni, Nadia. 1986. *La Prose: Oeuvres complètes*. Ed. Jad Hatem. Beirut: Dar An-Nahar.

————. 1986. *Les Oeuvres poétiques complètes*. Ed. Jad Hatem. Beirut: Dar An-Nahar.

The Night Sun

JAD HATEM

❧The metaphor of the "night sun" is unique insofar as it exhibits the borders at the center of things.[1] Although the moon is neither sun nor night, it depends on the former for its luminosity and on the latter for the occasion of its appearance. Therefore, to refer to the moon as the "night sun" is to reveal its composition and its contradictory attire, without expressing its essence. On one hand, this "sun" represents freedom through death's example; on the other, the "sun" seems either to substitute for love or to manifest love through its oxymoronic nature. This metaphor is reminiscent of the following line from the *Song of Songs*: "For love is strong as death." One noun easily substitutes for the other. Furthermore, love unites the self with the loved one. As passion, love is an infliction. Under these conditions, the freedom of the nocturnal sun can be figuratively interpreted as a release from all relationships, a release occurring at sunset, at the very moment the "disappearing" sun (always a negative in Tuéni's poetry) is replaced by the moon. The sunset is the dawn of freedom, an awakening, and opens the door for a night that allows for the indisputable centering around, and meditation on, the self. For death to appear as this dark sky bathed in moonlight, it is necessary not only for the soul to remain intact throughout the body's dismemberment but also for the self to endure in its role as a mobile center, illuminating during its stellar voyage while free of any external constraints. In other words, this condition in no way is congruent with biological death; for this reason, the suggestion of love's renewal (rather than its simple substitution) is important and should not be minimized. As a copula, love unites sun and night,

1. In this essay, Jad Hatem comments on the poem, "Oh Nocturnal weavings" ("O Nuits élaborées"), which can be found on pp. 58–59 of this edition.

self and profundity—a union that is freedom in death. But which kind of freedom? Prolonged contraction within oneself at the moment of the poetic act, for the "I" is coming.

What, then, is a moon? A "nocturnal weaving"! Affect asserting itself again in the poetic act! As a figure of original essence, as the point where all begins (the "Orient"), as the pale light illuminating things before Creation, the moon is revealed here through the open blank spaces allowed for by the breakdown of the meter, the scansion of the poem (and its typography). For this journey travelers are required, the self remaining lucid in the very midst of its audacity. The "courtesies" of the night are the poems. Rather, one should say largesses, as they are so numerous: as numerous as the year is counted in days (the "fingers")! What better to ask for than a daily offering, consisting of the supreme tactfulness of time that destroys us? So why, then, these largesses? Because in its poetic resonances can be heard an implicit rhyme with a phonetically related term: "poetess"!

Now that I have assessed the result of this poetic process, let me analyze how it develops. Wind has traditionally been associated archetypally with inspiration and the word "spirit" and by extension the concepts of "breath" and "God." But inspiration is ordinarily perceived as the penetration of an external word (Muse, Angel, or Demon of poetry) deep within a soul, which then utters two intermingled words in a single meter (a "mingled measure," as Coleridge says in *Kubla Khan*). But the internal configuration of the archetype is inverted in this poem insofar as the wind opens up, thus presenting itself not as a fertilizing element but, on the contrary, as an element to be fecundated—a manner of insinuating that the theme of this poem is poetry itself. As for these allies of the wind, their identities cannot be assigned with certainty, but it is nevertheless possible to imagine that among them are to be found these two: stormy passions or, better yet, poets themselves, inasmuch as an "alliance" already unites them with the spirit that draws them into its spiral! In order for the poetic process to generate a poem, the wind must open itself up; but in order for the poems to come into existence at all, poets must open themselves up!

And within this poetic penetration (or irruption) into the world-poetry (the equivalent in *Kubla Khan* of the original circumscription of the world, i.e., "girdled round"), words are put into direct communication with one another: "all speaks of all" on the condition that first "all speaks" *to* "all." The linking of word and thing is so weakened that in the play of tension between words joining and dispersing, the naming of the soul derives both its strength and significance from the undisclosed image. The chief mode of communication in this poem involves these two consecutive events: (1) liberation preceding any deliberation, and (2) universal correspondence. The first moment causes words to speak to one another, the second directs the soul to the spoken word. The word "all" designates, then, "beyond the totality of singulars" (be they words or things), the communion of two unitotalities of language and the soul brought into fertile contact with one another. This communion is precisely what the following line from the poems hastens to represent: "The sounds I imagine are rivers or sobs." The intermingling of these terms induces, through the alternation of echoes, a roar followed by a murmur, each an audible sound but one which, while tending towards form, has barely allowed itself to be informed, "ceaseless turmoil seething," as Coleridge puts it. The gasping for breath that is a simple rhythm until put into an image through exclusion and coalescence—exclusion because the sounds are rivers and sobs only through the renunciation, for example, of "cries" and "thunder"—coalescence because of its highly significant bifurcated form. The counterpart to a river (a worldly "thing") is the sob, an expression of affect. The sounds refer to flowing water or a tearful moan because of decisions made by the poetic "I" in the grips of dialogue within the poetry-world. The choice, then, is between one type or the other—a poetry of the world or a poetry of the soul. The poem has chosen not to choose because it projects its light onto the faculty of imagination and makes it susceptible to difference, indeed, to opposites—unless, of course, we imagine this duality by superimposing equally one conjunction upon the other; for the reader who reads the "or" likewise understands an *and*. Through their potential union, the sob is capable of saying something about the essence of the river (which is exactly what Coleridge does by blurring the woman mourning her demon lover at the gushing fountain with the labored breathing of the earth) and its reverse, i.e., the sacred stream darkens in tumult toward a lifeless ocean. Each is "river" or "sob" if the poet desires them to be in his/her response to the poetic material rising from the poetry-world. In the end, as the poet transmutes his/her poetry into a work of art, the pale and fragile light inherent to his/her poetry (like that which the moon writes on things) is strong enough to help the reader seize, deeply beyond the tension between the wounds/scars left open by the poet and the wind, a gaze at the poetic self "as at that instant when each observes the other."

Every poetic act is a recovering of affectivity, that is, perception by the poet of his essence. A truth is uttered by the poem only at the very moment it is written. But at "that instance" each poetic act is "affectively seized," that is, perception of the poet by his/her essence. However, this truth is uttered only by another poem embedded in the poem: the poem in the making, at the very moment it is being written. But that instant is likewise the one in which the poem is best read. Thus through the grace of the poem, the reader, whose own emotions are aroused and whose affectivity has been seized and expressed in the language of another, is his/her own observer and is revealed to him/herself. Through this process (after the contemplation of, and meditation on, him/herself), the reader is able to retain what is revealed—following the formation of the French verb *regarder* ("to watch"), derived from *garder* ("to retain," "keep," "watch over somebody"), and *garde* (v. 11, "kept").

The two final lines appear to be the conclusion of a carefully constructed argument. But what does this conclusion achieve? A guard or guarding. A country is locked away underneath the tongue. The association with prison, or at least with the idea of containment, is attenuated by the verb "kept [it]" in which protection is suggested. By lying underneath and not directly on the tongue, the country is prevented from being figuratively swallowed. The poet takes care *(prend garde)* within herself not to re-ingest the fruit of poetic experience (as pure affect) that cannot be given as such to others. Here, the poetic experience is uttered in the language of the word, the language meant for all. Yet, it has not been communicated outside the mouth. On the one hand, it has not left the writer's room because the poem is still being written; on the other, there is an element of privacy in the retention of the host, a retention deriving from a hesitation of saying to all that which would not be said to a close friend. The host's retention also springs from a fear that the poem might not be able to respond on its own account during the reading process, or worse, to defend itself in the absence of its author (as Plato said of all writing in *Phaedrus*).

Consider a passage from Victor Hugo's poem "Religio" found in his *Contemplations* in which the nocturnal star is described as "an enormous Host"("une énorme hostie") held by a priest, who is none other than God at the moment of the Elevation. In Hugo's poem, the image of the Host almost completely disappears, just as a piece of writing almost completely erases another on a palimpsest. But Tuéni's moon is protected, at least briefly, from any sacred display of the Host, from an Elevation that would change its very nature. It is comforting to recall its woven or even combined nature; the Host is the result of a marriage between nature and culture, the joint action of the soul's virginal spontaneity and the more deliberate work of the pen. In Tuéni's poem, the outcome involves itself in a secondary process, transubstantiation, because the work of the pen alone is incapable of producing the poem. For the pen's incapacity, Tuéni does not have recourse to either Rilke's angel or to Homer's muse. Instead she refers to the eternal Word, not because she makes any claims of inspiration through divine prophecy but because the poem itself is modeled on Christ, specifically, it carries within itself two natures that, indissolubly linked, are dependent upon the spontaneity of the initial act. The primary substance produced by the confluence of affect and the act of writing is not yet a poem if it is already reality. This murmur during which "all speaks of all" presents itself to the Word as matter to be transformed. But instead of this matter being transformed either into the work's *caput mortuum* (residue or refuse that is eliminated) or into the poem (the philosopher's stone), it participates in a recovery of the poem's poetological truth. And what does it speak of? Of the consul's garden and of evenings spent in gossiping and confabulation; of a country called either Lebanon or death in which at any moment anything can happen. Thought seeks itself by pecking away at its justification within the world. But those things that surrender to the poetry-world (and their babble) keep only their nominal appearance and are no longer given life by the poet's intention—except as these things point toward another revelation, specifically, the revelation of another substance (the soul united with the Word). This revelation, however, is not evident at a glance. The Host shines in vain inside a monstrance modeled after the sun; only the eye of faith is made privy to its true nature. And as for the poem? It tastes like bread, but can one see into its victim-like essence? The "night sun" is free as death for having been free for death.

Selected Bibliography

Adonis ['Ali Ahmad Sa'd]. *Introduction à la poétique arabe.* Paris: Sinbad, 1985; trans. as *Introduction to Arab Poetics.* Austin: Univ. of Texas Press, 1990.

Anhoury, Najwa Aoun. *Panorama de la poésie libanaise d'expression française.* Beirut: Dar El-Machreq, 1987.

Beydoun, Ahmad. *Liban: Itinéraires dans une guerre incivile.* Paris and Amman: Karthala and CERMOC, 1993.

Bonnefoy, Yves. *L'Arrière-pays.* Paris and Geneva: Flammarion and Skira, 1972.

Chedid, Andrée. *Terre et poésie.* Paris: Editions Guy Lévi Mano, 1956.

Cooke, Miriam. *War's Other Voices: Women Writers on the Lebanese Civil War.* Cambridge: Cambridge University Press, 1987.

Fakhouri, Nelly H. *La Quaternité de la parole poétique de Nadia Tuéni.* Beirut: Editions Dar An-Nahar, 1998.

Hatem, Jad. *La Quête poétique de Nadia Tuéni.* Beirut: Editions Dar An-Nahar, 1986.

Jabbour, Zahida Darwiche. *Poésie et Initiation chez Nadia Tuéni.* Beirut: Editions Dar An-Nahar, 1992.

Kristeva, Julia. *La Révolution du langage poétique.* Paris: Editions du Seuil, 1974.

Tuéni, Ghassan. *Une guerre pour les autres.* Paris: Jean-Claude Lattès, 1985.

Tuéni, Nadia. *Archives sentimentales d'une guerre au Liban* Paris: Editions Pauvert, 1982.

———. *Au-delà du regard.* Béirut: Editions Dar An-Nahar, 1986.

———. *De ma fenêtre sans maison.* Paris: Editions du Chêne, 1995.

———. *Jardin de ma mémoire. Anthologie.* Paris: Flammarion, 1998.

———. *Juin et les mécréantes.* Paris: Seghers, 1968.

———. *July of My Remembrance and Other Poems Translated from French.* Beirut: Editions Dar An-Nahar, n.d.

———. *L'Âge d'écume.* Paris: Seghers, 1965.

———. *La Terre arrêtée* Paris: Belfond, 1984.

———. *Le Rêveur de Terre.* Paris: Seghers, 1975.

————. *Les Textes blonds.* Beirut: Editions Dar An-Nahar, 1963.

————. *Liban: Vingt poèmes pour un amour.* Beirut: Dar An-Nahar, 1979. First translated in English as *Lebanon: Twenty Poems for One Love* by Samuel Hazo. New York: Byblos Press, 1990.

————. *Oeuvres complètes.* Complete Works: Volume I: Poetry; Volume II: Prose. Edited by Jad Hatem. Beirut: Editions Dar An-Nahar (Collection Patrimoine), 1986. Copyright Fondation Nadia Tuéni—Dar An-Nahar, 1986.

————. *Poèmes pour une histoire.* Paris: Seghers, 1972.

Vanhese, Gisèle. "Poète, passeur de frontières: sur l'oeuvre de Nadia Tuéni." Beirut: Fondation Nadia Tuéni, 1998.

————, trans. *Terra Immobile.* Italy: Sugarco Editions, 2000 (with collaboration of Fondation Nadia Tuéni).

Voss-Wittig, Huberta von, trans. *Janseits des Blickes.* Freiburg: Herder, 2000 (with collaboration of Fondation Nadia Tuéni); Hans Schiler Verlag, 2004.

About the Poet

Nadia Tuéni (1935–1983) received numerous awards for her poetry during her lifetime, including the Order of La Pléiade and the Prix Said Akl. She was also active in political circles, during periods after the June 1967 war and when her husband Ghassan was representative of the city of Beirut and Lebanon's ambassador to the UN. Most of her works were published in France by Pierre Seghers. She received a prestigious award from the French Academy in 1973 for *Poèmes pour une histoire* (Poems for a Story). In January 1999, a play based on a collection of poems about the 1967 Arab-Israeli war, *Juin et les mécréantes* (June and the Miscreants), was successfully performed in Paris. Tuéni's complete works (poetry and prose), as well as three book-length critical studies of her poetry, have been published in French by Dar An-Nahar, an internationally recognized Lebanese Francophone publisher. Many of her poems appear in foreign language anthologies, through French, English, Arabic, or Spanish translations. Translations of her works have also appeared in separate works by Gisèle Vanhese in Italian and by Huberta von Voss Wittig in German. Nadia Tuéni is the mother of Gebran and Makram Tuéni, born in 1957 and 1965 respectively.

1935   Born on July 8 in Baakline (Lebanon), daughter of Mohamed Ali Hamadé, Lebanese writer and diplomat, and Marguerite Malaquin. She attended secondary school in Beirut and was educated in the Druze religion.

1950   Studies in Greece, where her father was the Lebanese ambassador.

1954   Marries Ghassan Tuéni, journalist and representative of the city of Beirut to the Lebanese Parliament.

1962   Death of her daugher Nayla (born 1955) from cancer.

1963   Publication of her first poetry collection, *Les Textes blonds* (Beirut: Editions Dar An-Nahar).

1965   Discovers that she suffers from cancer.

1965   *L'Âge d'écume* (Paris: Seghers).

1967   Literary editor at the Francophone Lebanese newspaper *Le Jour* (currently *L'Orient-Le Jour*); intense political and literary activity.

1968   *Juin et les mécréantes* (Paris: Seghers).

1972   *Poèmes pour une histoire* (Paris: Seghers).
       Winner of the 1973 French Academy Prize.

1975   *Le Rêveur de Terre* (Paris: Seghers). Translated into Arabic in 1983.

1976   Recipient of "l'Ordre de la Pléiade," an award given in Paris to Francophone writers promoting dialogue between cultures.

1979   *Liban: Vingt Poèmes pour un amour* (Beirut: Editions Dar An-Nahar). First translated in English by Samuel Hazo as *Lebanon: Twenty Poems for One Love* (New York: Byblos Press, 1990). Some poems of this collection appeared in *The Atlantic Review.*

1982   *Archives sentimentales d'une guerre au Liban* (Paris: Editions Pauvert). Translated into Arabic in 1983 (Beirut: Editions Dar An-Nahar).

1983   Nadia Tuéni dies from cancer on June 20.

1984   *La Terre arrêtée* (Paris: Belfond). A collection of posthumous unpublished poems, which also includes homages from Georges Schehadé and Andrée Chedid. A recording of *Archives sentimentales d'une guerre au Liban,* interpreted by Jean-Louis Barrault, Alain Cuny, Geneviève Page, Sylvia Monfort, and Delphine Seyrig, was produced in Paris.

1986   *Au-delà du regard.* Beirut: Editions Dar An-Nahar.

1986   Oeuvres complètes *[Complete Works: Volume I: Poetry; Volume II: Prose].* Edited by Jad Hatem. Beirut: Dar An-Nahar. Volume II (prose) includes essays on poetry, politics, Druze religion, and theater. It also includes three short stories.

Contributors

Jad Hatem is professor and former chair of philosophy at Saint-Joseph University, Beirut. He is the editor of Nadia Tuéni's complete works in French and author of *La Quête poétique de Nadia Tuéni*. A celebrated poet, his most recent books include *L'Audace pascale, La Mystique de Gibran et le supra-confessionalisme religieux des chrétiens d'Orient, Mal d'amour et joie de la poésie, Par la poussière des étoiles.*

The author of books of poetry, fiction, essays and plays, **Samuel Hazo** is the founder and director of the International Poetry Forum in Pittsburgh, Pennsylvania. He is also McAnulty Distinguished Professor of English Emeritus at Duquesne University, where he taught for forty-two years. Some of his previous books are *The Holy Surprise of Right Now* and *As They Sail* (poetry), *Stills* (fiction), *Feather* and *Mano a Mano* (drama), and *Spying for God* (essays). His translations include Denis de Rougemont's *The Growl of Deeper Waters,* Nadia Tuéni's *Lebanon: Twenty Poems for One Love,* and Adonis' *The Pages of Day and Night.* His latest book of poems, *Just Once: New and Previous Poems,* received the Maurice English Poetry Award in 2003, and a new collection of poems entitled *A Flight to Elsewhere* was published in 2005. He was most recently honored with the Griffin Award for Creative Writing from the University of Notre Dame, his alma mater. A National Book Award finalist, he was chosen the first State Poet of the Commonwealth of Pennsylvania by Governor Robert Casey in 1993, and he served in that capacity until 2003.

Syrine C. Hout is associate professor of English and comparative literature at the American University of Beirut. She is the author of *Viewing Europe from the Outside* and numerous studies of travel narratives and cross-cultural theory. Her current interest in contemporary Lebanese fiction produced in exile has resulted in journal articles and book chapters on several writers of note, including Rabih Alameddine, Tony Hanania, Hani Hammoud, Nada Awar Jarrar, Emily Nasrallah, and Hanan al-Shaykh.

Christophe Ippolito is assistant professor of French at the University of the Pacific in Stockton, California. He has published essays on nineteenth- and twentieth-century French and Francophone literature and culture. His most recent book is entitled *Narrative Memory in Flaubert's Works.*

Paul B. Kelley, author of translations of Deleuze, has published essays on Samuel Beckett, Proust, Sartre, and Céline. His most recent book is entitled *Stories for Nothing: Samuel Beckett's Narrative Poetics.*